THE
THRIFTY GUIDE TO
ANCIENT ROME

A HANDBOOK FOR TIME TRAVELERS

THE
THRIFTY GUIDE TO
ANCIENT ROME

A HANDBOOK FOR TIME TRAVELERS

Jonathan W. Stokes
illustrated by David Sossella

VIKING

VIKING

Penguin Young Readers

An imprint of Penguin Random House LLC

375 Hudson Street

New York, New York 10014

First published in the United States of America by Viking,

an imprint of Penguin Random House LLC, 2018

LIBRARY OF CONGRESS CATALOGING-IN-PUBLICATION DATA

Names: Stokes, Jonathan W., author. | Sossella, David, illustrator.

Title: The thrifty guide to ancient Rome: a handbook for time travelers / by Jonathan W. Stokes ; illustrated by David Sossella.

Description: New York : Penguin Group, 2017. | Series: The thrifty guides | Audience: Grades 4–6. | Audience: Ages 8–12.

Identifiers: LCCN 2017006306 (print) | LCCN 2017007298 (ebook) | ISBN 9781101998083 (hardcover) | ISBN 9780451479600 (paper-over-board) | ISBN 9781101998120 (ebook)

Subjects: LCSH: Rome—Civilization—Juvenile literature.

Classification: LCC DG77 .S83 2017 (print) | LCC DG77 (ebook) | DDC 937—dc23 LC record available at https://lccn.loc.gov/2017006306

Manufactured in China   Book design, maps, and graphs by Mariam Quraishi

1   3   5   7   9   10   8   6   4   2

PREFACE

The Thrifty Guide to Ancient Rome: A Handbook for Time Travelers was published holographically by Time Corp in the year 2163. It presents a complete vacation package for tourists visiting ancient Rome. A careless time traveler accidentally left a copy of this handy guidebook in our own era, where it was picked up by a New York publishing house. The result is the book you are now reading.

Researchers suspect that in the future Time Corp will publish many editions of the Thrifty Guide series, including guides for ancient Greece, medieval times, and the American Revolution. It seems Time Corp will acquire most of North America in a hostile takeover sometime around 2150. As of yet, we know very little about Time Corp's corporate overlord, Finn Greenquill, except that his lawyers are too disorganized to prevent us from republishing this book.

The Thrifty Guide to Ancient Rome contains information vital to the sensible time traveler:

Where can I find a decent hotel room in ancient Rome for under five sesterces a day? Is horse parking included?

What do I do if I'm attacked by barbarians?

What are my legal options if I'm fed to the lions at the Colosseum?

All this is answered and more. There is handy advice on finding the best picnicking spots to watch Julius Caesar's assassination at the Roman Forum in 44 BC, as well as helpful real estate tips to profit from the great Roman fire of AD 64. There are even useful recommendations on which famous historical figures to meet for lunch, and a few nifty pointers on how to avoid being poisoned, beheaded, or torn apart by an angry mob.

What follows is the guidebook, exactly as it was discovered on a sidewalk outside Frank's Pizza in Manhattan in AD 2018. . . .

THE THRIFTY GUIDE TO ANCIENT ROME
A HANDBOOK FOR TIME TRAVELERS

TIME CORP!™ SERVING YESTERDAY, FOR A BETTER TOMORROW, TODAY.™

MAP OF TIME CORP HEADQUARTERS IN NEW NEW NEW NEW NEW NEW NEW YORK, AD 2163

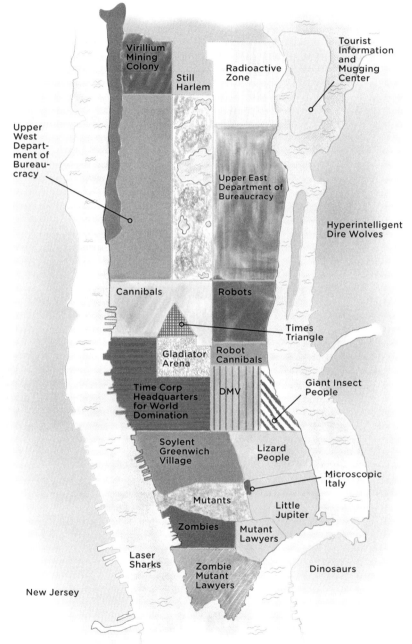

Virillium Mining Colony

Still Harlem

Radioactive Zone

Tourist Information and Mugging Center

Upper West Department of Bureaucracy

Upper East Department of Bureaucracy

Hyperintelligent Dire Wolves

Cannibals

Robots

Times Triangle

Gladiator Arena

Robot Cannibals

Giant Insect People

Time Corp Headquarters for World Domination

DMV

Soylent Greenwich Village

Lizard People

Microscopic Italy

Mutants

Little Jupiter

Zombies

Mutant Lawyers

Laser Sharks

Zombie Mutant Lawyers

Dinosaurs

New Jersey

IMPORTANT WARNINGS BEFORE TIME TRAVELING

1. If you time travel to a moment immediately before you time travel, you may be caught in an infinite time loop.

2. If you are caught in an infinite time loop, we refer you to our 24-hour customer service line on Omega Five. It is called a 24-hour customer service line because you can expect hold times of at least 24 hours.

3. Hey, don't sweat the long hold times, buddy. This is why we have time machines.

4. If you purchase this book, travel back in time, and give yourself this book in order to avoid having to purchase it, the Time Patrol may put you in jail before even sentencing you.

5. Hunt barbarians at your own risk.

6. Word to the wise: don't have lunch with Julius Caesar; he never picks up the tab.

CONTENTS

INTRODUCTION
THE BASICS OF TIME TRAVEL

1. The Problem with the Future

Those of us clever enough to be born in the twenty-second century lead perfect lives. School, for instance, can be a rough period in life . . . unless you have a time machine and can skip it altogether. Then you can focus on the good parts, like vacations, which you can live over and over again.

Didn't study for the big exam? No problem, you have a time machine. Didn't think of the right joke on the spur of the moment? Fire up that time machine. Chose the wrong career and lived a life full of regret? *Buenos días,* time machine!

Of course, this all made life somewhat complicated once time machines became household appliances in AD 2149. Somehow, *everyone* began picking the winning lottery numbers. *Everyone* threw game-winning touchdowns. And *everyone* nailed their job interviews. Suddenly, *everyone* was fantastically wealthy, which led to inflation. And *everyone* was fantastically happy, which was just obnoxious.

All this led to the great economic collapse of 2150, in which everyone became so poor they had to sell their time machines.[*] But we digress.

The point is, people in the past led difficult lives. Those poor chumps were forced to fight wars because they didn't already know the outcome. They needed to come up with new ideas using creativity, rather than just copying ideas from the future. And they still experienced even the most basic health problems, like death.

All this means that the past is an infinitely more interesting time period than our own. So grab your iridium blaster, stamp your past-port, and enjoy your vacation to yesteryear. And always remember: leave no trace, and try not to start any wars that weren't supposed to be started.

2. The Nature of Time Travel

Scientists used to believe there were infinite possible timelines, leading to infinite possible worlds, which meant there were infinite scientists in infinite worlds, working on infinite theories of time. Following this logic, scientists began billing their universities for infinite overtime. So the universities quickly scrapped this entire theory.

Now most scientists believe there is only one timeline, so we had better not muck it up. If you travel back in time and shoot

....
*Incidentally, this is when Time Corp was able to buy most of America in a hostile takeover.

yourself before you traveled back in time, the ensuing paradox will be so maddening, it will make you want to travel back in time and shoot yourself.

Some scientists believe there may still be infinite possible worlds, though all scientists agree there is no possible world in which you can catch a cab during rush hour in Manhattan. Time Corp's stellar legal department has managed to secure sole publishing rights to this travel guide in at least one thousand of these possible worlds.

3. Time Patrol

When you go back in time, you will almost certainly botch the timeline of world history. Not to worry. The dedicated men and women of the Time Patrol will carefully review your vacation itinerary and take all steps necessary to clean up any damage you've done to history during your trip. Time Corp guarantees you will retain all memories and photos of your travels, or you get your money back.

4. Your Time Machine

The 2163 Time Corp Time Machine Sedan™ is the new gold standard in luxury time travel. Four doors, all-wood paneling, a moonroof, all-leather interior, fully reclining seats, 11.1 Stereo

Surround Sound, and a one-year warranty.* It is a model of fuel efficiency, burning only 795 metric tons of carbon per trip. At the current gas price of $995 per gallon, this is a steal!

The Time Machine Sedan™ is fully equipped with air bags. If you somehow create a rift in the space-time continuum, the air bags will provide a gentle, cushioning sensation in the last millisecond of time before your molecules are blasted across thousands of parsecs of space in an earth-shattering explosion.

Congratulations, you are now ready to begin your journey!

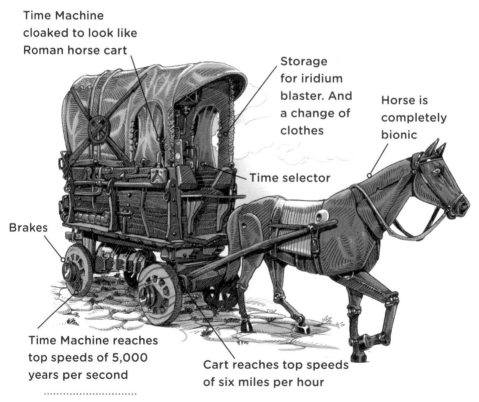

Time Machine cloaked to look like Roman horse cart

Storage for iridium blaster. And a change of clothes

Horse is completely bionic

Time selector

Brakes

Time Machine reaches top speeds of 5,000 years per second

Cart reaches top speeds of six miles per hour

*Time Corp's legal team admits it is extremely easy to void a one-year warranty when traveling thousands of years through time. From what year in space-time do we measure the year of warranty? We honestly have no idea.

1

WELCOME TO ROME

WHETHER YOU ARE traveling solo or taking advantage of one of Time Corp's very affordable group packages, Rome is a magical getaway for you and your loved ones, provided you are not attacked by barbarians.* Drop by the city on December 7, 43 BC, and watch as the Roman Senator Cicero's head is chopped off and tastefully displayed on the main podium of the Roman Forum. Enjoy a quiet weekend retreat in the mountainside town of Pompeii in AD 79, shortly before it is incinerated in a massive volcanic eruption. Or revel in the stunning views of southern Italy's many sun-soaked beaches in 280 BC, unless they are being stormed by rampaging Greeks. Yes, nothing says "relaxing getaway" quite like vacationing in the colorful civilization that gave us lawyers, martial law, civil war, tax fraud, and gladiator fights. Say what you will about the rioting mobs or pillaging invaders; when in Rome, there is never a dull moment.

....

*During your stay in the Roman Empire, Time Corp is not responsible for attacks by ancient Persians, Gauls, Germans, Goths, or Vandals. If, however, Rome is attacked by Mars colonists from AD 2351, Time Corp might actually be somehow responsible. In which case, please accept our deepest apologies . . . as well as an eight dollar coupon toward your next Time Corp vacation!

ROMAN EMPIRE IN AD 120
(ABOUT 2,000 YEARS AGO)

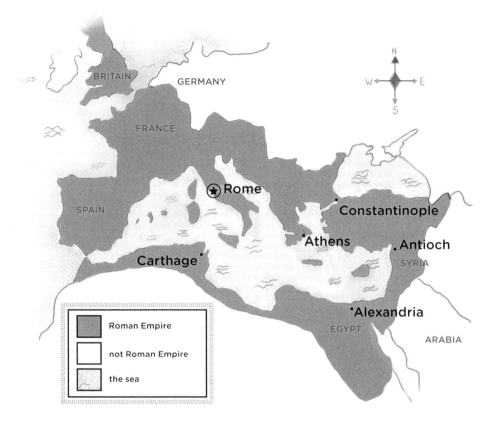

Rome is the capital city of the Roman Empire,[*] which stretches across three continents. Founded in 753 BC, nearly three thousand years ago, Rome became the first great superpower in Western history. You are about to experience the civilization that changed the art, literature, laws, and government of the modern world. If you set your time machine to AD 30 and enter the city

....

*Finn Greenquill, who is an absolute stickler for detail, insists we point out that Rome doesn't truly become an empire until 27 BC, when it is ruled by Emperor Augustus. Before then, Rome is a republic ruled by Senators. We asked Finn, "Who cares? Why does anyone need to know this?" But he signs our paychecks.

along one of Rome's twenty-nine paved highways, you will find a thriving metropolis crammed with merchants, architects, soldiers, Senators, slaves, farmers, lawyers, scribes, and all manner of tradesmen. Rome is the first city in history to reach one million inhabitants. In fact, it takes another two thousand years before any other city on earth reaches this size.[*]

A city this big can be a bit intimidating. Sure, it's the cultural center of the ancient world. But you'll want to keep your cash hidden and a sharp eye out for thieves. Rome is a dangerous place, even when it's not getting pillaged by Visigoths, Ostrogoths, or any other kind of Goth. This chapter focuses on the basics you'll need to get settled. Where to find food, lodging, and transportation, all without getting yourself killed. In fact, let's start with that part. . . .

Not Getting Killed in Ancient Rome

A primary goal of any pleasant vacation is to not get yourself killed.[†] This is easier said than done. Rome is an absolute death trap.

....

[*]London hits one million by AD 1801. Alexandria, Egypt; Hangzhou, China; and Angkor, Cambodia, may all have reached one million people prior to London, but London is the first city to leave us reliable census data. If you visit any of these other cities, please count how many people live in them.

[†]Those of you particularly keen on not dying may want to avoid Time Corp's travel package to the Middle Ages. We especially do not recommend the "Black Death Getaway Package." It's for only our most adventuresome travelers . . . or for our budget travelers who absolutely cannot afford anything better.

TOP FIVE WAYS TO DIE IN ROME

1. Fire

If you are a pyromaniac, Rome is the place to be. Fires break out so frequently, you can grab a snack, climb up on your roof, and watch the town burn. Homes burn down nearly every night, an entire neighborhood burns down every two years, and the en-

tire city burns down completely in AD 64. This is because open fires and olive oil lamps are the only source of fuel and light. In its early days, for bonus flammability, many of Rome's buildings are wooden structures with thatched straw roofs, built incredibly close together. If you are trying to build a combustible city, you can't do better than Rome with this winning combination of open flames and a complete lack of fire codes. If you're visiting Rome, bring marshmallows.

2. Flood

Time Corp's legal department requires us to mention that if the fires don't kill you, the floods probably will. The Tiber River provides Rome with transportation and trade, but regularly drowns Romans by flooding its banks a few times a year. In severe floods, the Tiber may surge 30 feet above its normal level, carrying

entire apartment buildings downstream. When your apartment collapses, you're going to have a bad time. Perhaps most disturbingly, Rome's sewage system is tied to the water level. So every time there's a flood, many of Rome's toilets back up and empty into the streets. Don't say we didn't warn you.

3. Famine

Famine is a regular visitor to Rome. Every time there is a bad flood, the grain supply rots and Romans starve. When the floods are deep enough, the grain warehouses, conveniently built along the Tiber River, are carried away entirely. When you're heading to Rome, maybe pack a few extra sandwiches just in case. Couldn't hurt.

4. Disease

Stroll down a Roman street and you will probably notice a stench so overpowering you'll think your eyes will start bleeding. While Rome has the most sophisticated system of aqueducts in history, and the most technologically advanced water supply system the world will see for another two thousand years, the city's sewers are not quite up to modern-day standards. Many of the streets are, for lack of better words, toilets and graveyards. Lots of Romans simply empty their waste by tossing it out the front door. Homeless people die in the streets, and each year some 1,500 bodies are left to rot. The city's horses, cows, goats, and mules all defecate and die in the streets as well. Some friendly advice: don't wear your favorite shoes when you're visiting Rome. You may,

however, wish to wear a hat; many Roman lawsuits are recorded from pedestrians being struck on the head by human waste flung out of chamber pots from fourth-story windows.

All of this waste is a breeding ground for disease. One out of every three babies born in Rome promptly dies in Rome. Fully 50 percent of children die before they become teenagers. The only way Rome is able to maintain its population is through immigration. It just goes to show you, no matter how deadly a city is, certain people are always willing to move there—much like modern-day Los Angeles.*

Rome is conveniently built in a swamp, where disease-carrying mosquitoes can breed and multiply. Every autumn, Rome's death toll spikes as mosquito-borne malaria ravages the city. Before visit-

....

*Time Corp's legal department wishes to point out that the writer of this paragraph actually lives in Los Angeles.

ing the architectural wonders of ancient Rome, make sure you get your shots.[*]

5. Angry Mobs

We should also mention the roving, rampaging mobs. During the food riots[†] in AD 190, the emperor Commodus has his chief adviser's head torn off and thrown into the streets to appease the angry mob. Farther south, in 73 BC, a Thracian[‡] gladiator named Spartacus leads a revolt of ninety thousand slaves who take over much of Italy before being massacred by the Roman military. When the Roman leader Julius Caesar is assassinated in 44 BC, the mob becomes so enraged they burn down the Senate. As a general rule: try to keep clear of rioting mobs, or at least remember to bring pepper spray.

Okay, we know what you're thinking. *Why should anyone want to visit Rome?*

That's a fair question. We probably should have led the chapter with that part. Well, you're here in Rome now, and Time Corp doesn't give refunds. So you might as well get used to it. The fact that you might die at any moment is exactly why Time Corp has

....

[*]Time Corp's corporate overlord, Finn Greenquill, would like to remind you that Time Corp offers excellent deals on vaccinations. And failing that, funerals.

[†]A food riot is sort of the opposite of a food fight. Instead of having so much food you can fight people with it, you have so little food that you fight people for it.

[‡]The Thracians are barbarians from what is now Bulgaria, with red hair, blue eyes, and a penchant for warfare.

made this travel package *very attractively priced*. On the other hand, Rome contributes an astonishing amount to human civilization. European languages such as English, French, Spanish, Italian, and even Romanian are all based on or influenced by Roman Latin. The Romans have the most advanced medicine in the ancient world. Modern government, literature, law, architecture, sports, military structure, holidays, art, and even poetry owe a staggering amount to Roman culture. Rome is one of our most exciting travel packages, and Time Corp guarantees you are going to have a good time.[*]

----

[*]You are legally required to have a good time, according to the contract you signed when you bought this vacation package. In fact, Finn Greenquill would like to remind you that you are required to give Time Corp excellent, five-star reviews on all review sites, most of which are owned by Time Corp.

MAP OF PLACES WHERE PEOPLE GET KILLED (A.K.A. ROME)

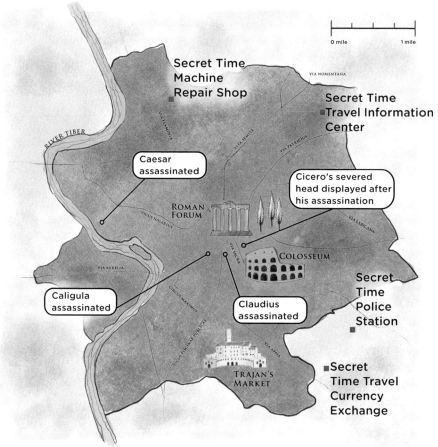

0 mile   1 mile

Secret Time Machine Repair Shop

Secret Time Travel Information Center

VIA NOMENTANA

RIVER TIBER

VIA FLAMINIA

ALTA SEMITA

VIA PATRICIUS

Caesar assassinated

Cicero's severed head displayed after his assassination

ROMAN FORUM

VICUS IUGARIUS

VIA LABICANA

VIA SACRA

COLOSSEUM

VIA AURELIA

Caligula assassinated

CIRCUS MAXIMUS

Claudius assassinated

Secret Time Police Station

VICUS PISCINAE PUBLICAE

VIA APPIA

TRAJAN'S MARKET

Secret Time Travel Currency Exchange

Getting Around in Ancient Rome

Sure, the Greeks came up with the grid system, but the Romans took city planning to a whole new level. Nearly all Romans live in apartment buildings called *insulae*. These concrete apartment buildings are up to ten stories high and can take up entire city blocks. There are fifty thousand apartment buildings in Rome. They're fairly modern in many ways, except they have the unfortunate habit of collapsing.

By the empire's peak, Rome's 113 provinces are connected by 372 paved highways. That's more than 50,000 miles of paved roads, many of which survive for thousands of years. France alone contains 13,000 miles of Roman roadways.

If you're trying to blend into Roman society, hoverboards are surprisingly conspicuous. The best way to see the sights without upsetting the locals is on a horse.

HELPFUL HINTS:
HOW TO PILOT A HORSE

A horse is a grass-powered locomotion device.

1. Fly onto the horse using your antigravity boots.
2. Look down and you will see four spindly appendages with hooves at the bottom. These are the horse's propellers.
3. The horse's start button is located in its "flanks." Press it with your heels. The harder you press, the faster the horse will go.
4. The horse's controls are a metal bit located inside its mouth. You control this joystick with reins.
5. The horse's brakes are engaged by yanking on the reins. If all else fails, you can stop the horse by transporting it into a swamp.

More Helpful Hints

Horses cannot be steered by telepathy. Horses do not acquire telepathy until the year 2061, after the meteor crash. Horses do not require nuclear fission material. In fact, they run far better without it.

Refuel your horse by filling it with grass. Stuff the grass into the horse's mouth until the horse is filled. The mouth is the end that doesn't have a tail over it.

NOTE: Your horse cannot go airborne. Unless you attach rockets to it.

Looking Fabulous in Imperial Rome

The trickiest part about time travel isn't multidimensional physics; it's knowing what to wear. Show up in the Roman Forum with sunglasses, a cell phone,* and a skateboard, and the locals may assume you are some sort of witch, or worse yet, really unfashionable. If you want to blend in to ancient Rome, jeans and sneakers aren't going to cut the mustard. You're going to need a proper disguise. Follow these fashion tips and you'll be allowed into any restaurant in the city.

Romans take fashion very seriously. While any chump can wear a tunic, only free Roman citizens are allowed to wear togas. Any foreigner or slave caught wearing a toga is punished by law.

If you think you can pass as a citizen and you're planning to wear a toga, just know that it's been bleached white using stale urine. The ammonium salts in stale urine are a common bleaching agent that make your whites whiter. It was often the job of Roman fullers (cloth dyers) to go around the city draining urine from public street urinals in order to make bleach. Adding insult to injury, the urine collectors had to pay taxes on all the urine they collected. Yup, in Rome you have to *pay* for the right to scoop urine out of a urinal.

If you've got some shopping to do, Rome has enormous open street markets, known as forums. You can buy a whole

....

*Also, try not to use your cell phone in the ancient world too much; the roaming charges are *exorbitant*.

new wardrobe at Trajan's Market, a three-story precursor
to the modern shopping mall. It's located in the fancy Cap-
itoline neighborhood in the expensive heart of Rome, and
contains 170 storefronts. You may be overcharged, but don't
worry. One US dollar in 2163 is worth about ten thousand
Roman sesterces.

A HELPFUL FASHION GUIDE TO BLENDING INTO ANCIENT ROME

WOMEN

Tunic: a simple square garment pinned at the shoulder, often with fabric all the way to the feet

Stola: a sleeveless floor-length garment worn over the tunic by married women, often with a belt

Palla: a long cloak worn outside the house

Jewelry: earrings, necklaces, rings, pins, or bracelets

MEN

Tunic: tied with a belt, with stripes denoting one's rank in society. A man's tunic is shorter than a woman's.

Toga: a large cloth wrapped around the body and draped over the shoulder. Great for toga parties.

Jewelry: gold rings and neck chains will never go out of fashion in Italy

Sandals: open-toed sandals are sensible footwear for the Mediterranean climate

Roman Hairstyles

Every time traveler knows the horror of walking into a seventeenth-century ball wearing a sixteenth-century haircut. The trouble with humans is they're constantly changing fashions. Here are a few pointers on hairstyles, just so you don't show up in downtown Rome rocking a green mohawk.

MEN

Roman men wear their hair cropped short. Balding men often wear toupees made of human hair. Beards go in and out of fashion. Emperor Nero actually rocks a *neck beard*.

WOMEN

Wigs made of human hair are very popular, especially exotic colors from conquered barbarians. Blond hair imported from Germany or black hair imported from India are especially fashionable. Women and even men sometimes use curling irons, heating metal rods in a fire and wrapping their hair around the rods. Hair dye is also popular in ancient Rome. Here are *actual* dye recipes, as recorded by famous Romans:

Black hair dye: Let some leeches rot in a bowl of red wine for forty days.   —*Pliny the Elder,*[*] *Roman author*

Red hair dye: Mix goat fat with beechwood ashes.
                                        —*Pliny the Elder*

Blond hair dye: Saffron.
        —*Tertullian, author and son of a Roman centurion*

If you don't have time to visit a hairdresser while in ancient Rome, Time Corp sells several brands of hair dye that are very affordable and are almost 100 percent leech-free.

....

*Pliny the Elder dies from inhaling poisonous volcanic gas while trying to rescue friends from the deadly eruption at Pompeii. So he's clearly an expert on health and safety.

Places to Eat

If you don't have enough money for food, don't panic—you will only burn more calories. If worse comes to worst, the Roman government provides free grain to the poor. By 58 BC, Rome is doling out free grain to more than two hundred thousand members of the lower classes. While the wealthiest Romans dine on flamingo tongue soup, most Romans live on a diet of bread, olive oil, and wine.

A step up from free government bread is a visit to a thermopolium—a Roman fast-food joint. You wait in line and order your food at a walk-up counter facing the street. From there, you can either eat your ready-made meal on the go or on a sidewalk bench by the restaurant. Rome, Pompeii, Herculaneum, and Ostia all have excellent thermopolia worth trying. You can also grab snacks at the local *popina* or wine bar.

‖ CLODIUS'S FAST FOOD THERMOPOLIUM ‖

> **Food:** ★★
> **Noise Level:** Loud 👏👏👏
> **Decor:** ★
> **Wheelchair Accessible:** No ✗
> **Service:** ★
> **Accepts Credit Cards:** No ✗
> **Cost:** $ $ $ $
> **Attire:** No sandals, no service

What Clodius's restaurant lacks in ambiance, it makes up for with fast service. Hot food is served from steaming pots sunk into the counter. Granted, there are no sneeze-guards, but hey, you get what you pay for. There are chicken, lamb, and seafood dishes, as well as vegetable options. Clodius's specialty is baked cheese with honey. For a snack, try the nuts and dried fruit.*

Here is what some of our readers say about Clodius's Fast Food Thermopolium:

★★ "Try the sausages. Do not try the snails or oak grubs."
—Elaine S., Charleston, SC

★★★ "I would have given this restaurant four stars, but some Roman soldiers were eating at the counter, and when I mentioned that I'm part French, they tried to enslave me."
—Bob C., Omaha, NE

★★ "Clodius refused to take my American Express credit card. When I complained, he chased me out with a sword."
—Chad L., Albuquerque, NM

★★ "I'm just bummed the Italians don't invent pizza for another thousand years." —Tommy A., Brooklyn, NY

*As far as we know, no one has died from eating at Clodius's Fast Food Thermopolium. However, the Time Corp legal department insists we point out that Clodius paid Time Corp to include this restaurant review in the guidebook.

Public Bathrooms

Not to return too quickly to the topic of human waste, but after a trip to Clodius's Fast Food Thermopolium, you may find yourself in need of a restroom. You're in luck. By AD 315, Rome boasts 144 public bathrooms, all flushed clean by running water. The toilets are holes cut in a long slab of stone. Romans do not use toilet paper, but rather a sponge on a stick that rests beside each toilet in a trough of running water.

The bathrooms accommodate up to one hundred people at a time. There are no stalls for privacy. Romans just sit and chat while doing their business. If you are looking for the men's room, you won't find it. You won't find the women's room either. Rather, all men, women, and children use the same giant restroom together.

Public Roman bathrooms are frequented by rich and poor alike. So if you're a politician wishing to hobnob with voters, the bathroom is a great place to shake some hands . . . assuming your voters wash their hands. Similarly, if you're looking to borrow a few sesterces from a rich friend, the toilet is a great place to corner them.

Where to Stay in Ancient Rome

There are decent hotels along the major roadways, both in Rome and throughout the empire. A good hotel should provide straw bedding and ample space for you and any donkeys you may have. Granted, there is no running water, the highways are overrun with thieves, and buildings are prone to burn down anytime someone turns on a lamp. But prices are very reasonable. Also, you will have to take out your own sewage.

THE VESUVIUS INN

★★☆☆☆

Parking: Mule, horse, donkey (no valet parking)
Noise Level: Loud 👏 👏 👏
Attire: Semi-casual barbarian
Decor: ★ ★
Wheelchair Accessible: No ✕
Service: ★
Accepts Credit Cards: No ✕
Cost: $ $ $ $
Accepts Food for Barter: No ✕
Accepts Plunder: Yes ✓
Amenities: Bales of straw for donkeys
Wi-Fi: No ✕

The Vesuvius Inn is crowded, filthy, and dangerous, and those are its good points. There is a thermopolium on the first floor, with a few rooms for rent on the second floor. The Vesuvius provides convenient and affordable accommodations, as long as the fires from the kitchen aren't burning it down.

Here is what some of our readers say about the Vesuvius Inn:

★★ "I really enjoyed my stay at the hotel, until I was robbed by a bandit from Thracia." —Phyllis R., Jackson, WY

★ "The rooms were all filled up, so the hotel management made me sleep in the stable. I'm allergic to hay! Also, I was beaten up by a bandit from Thracia." —Hector M., Pomona, CA

★ "A bandit from Thracia ransacked my room and I got stuck with the cleaning bill. Also, the bandit stole my children and sold them to Moorish pirates." —Carmen L., Allentown, PA

★★★★★ "I had an excellent stay at this hotel." —A bandit from Thracia

2

ROMAN ENTERTAINMENT

WHEN YOU'RE IN ROME, you may be attacked, robbed, or chased by an angry mob, but you will never, ever be bored. Rome is full of entertainment choices for your viewing pleasure. For those with refined tastes, there is world-class theater, art, and even famous poets like Ovid, Virgil, and Horace who perform live in public. For those with less refined tastes, the Romans also enjoy a great variety of sports and spectacles, most of which involve witnessing violent death, all for a very attractive price. There are the chariot races where charioteers are killed, the gladiator matches where gladiators are killed, the beast hunts where wild animals are killed, and the spectacles where criminals are killed. So many wonderful options to choose from!

Gladiator Matches

If you really want to take advantage of all Rome has to offer, why not check out a gladiator match?

Roman gladiators fight wild animals, condemned criminals, or other gladiators, all for the entertainment of cheering crowds. This is largely because reality TV does not get invented until the twentieth century.

Most gladiators are European slaves or sentenced criminals, but a few are willing volunteers. Some of the most famous gladiators are women, others are dwarfs, and a few, including Caligula and Commodus, are emperors.

There are four hundred gladiator arenas throughout the Roman Empire at its height. If you want to become a gladiator and try your hand at combat, keep in mind that a gladiator's career almost never lasts more than ten matches.* Also, as a beginner,

---

*If you celebrate Christmas, you may want to keep that under your hat. Several Roman emperors, particularly Nero, get their kicks by feeding Christians to wild animals in the Colosseum.

your fee for your first match is only about one thousand sesterces.

Roughly eight thousand gladiators are killed per year across the empire. The average gladiator dies by age twenty-seven. On the upside, gladiators can become wildly famous and earn up to one hundred thousand sesterces per fight.

THE FLAVIAN AMPHITHEATER

★★☆☆☆

Food: ★
Noise Level: Deafening
Decor: ★★★
Wheelchair Accessible: No ✕
Service: ★
Accepts Credit Cards: No ✕
Cost: $ $ $ $
Attire: No knives

The Flavian Amphitheater is more popularly known as the Roman Colosseum. It is the ancestor of every sports stadium in the world. When you show your ticket, you're directed through one of eighty entrance gates, up four tiers of seating, and then to your row and assigned seat. The building is gigantic, holding fifty-five thousand spectators, and has a retractable canvas roof to provide shade.

Here's what some of our readers have to say about the Roman Colosseum:

★ "I paid fifty sesterces for my family's tickets, and they were all fed to the lions. I want my money back!"
—Roger G., Santa Fe, NM

★★ "I only got to see one family fed to the lions. I want my money back!"
—Bob R., Tampa, FL

★ "I only got to eat one family. And I want to go back to Africa."
—Lion

PEOPLE TO HAVE LUNCH WITH:
SPARTACUS

Spartacus is a gladiator who leads a slave rebellion that almost topples the Roman Republic in 73 BC. He is originally a Thracian mercenary who joins the Roman army, regrets his decision, and tries to desert. Spartacus is sold into slavery as a punishment. Like many slaves with size and strength, he is trained to become a gladiator.

The thing about training slaves to fight is it can come back to bite you. Spartacus and seventy of his fellow gladiators fight their way free and set about pillaging the Roman countryside. Eventually, some ninety thousand slaves join the uprising. The slaves score several stunning victories over the Roman army.

Finally Crassus, the richest man in Rome, uses his own money to raise legions of soldiers to fight Spartacus. During their final battle, Spartacus fights his way across the entire battlefield, kills both the centurions* guarding Crassus, but fails to kill Crassus himself. Spartacus is believed to be killed in this battle, though his body is never found.

Crassus wins a decisive victory, ending the revolt and capturing six thousand slaves. He crucifies all six thousand, leaving their bodies strung up on crosses along a 120-mile stretch of the Appian Way, the main highway to Rome.

Beast Hunts

Beast hunts are a popular form of entertainment where Romans can visit an arena and watch people hunt wild animals, watch wild animals hunt people, or watch wild animals hunt each other. Thousands of animals are killed in this way, and more than a few people. On April 21, AD 248, to celebrate the thousandth anniversary of Rome's founding, the Colosseum is home to the massacre of:

....

*A centurion is an army officer who commands a large group of soldiers. If you want to become a centurion, you need to be a skilled warrior, preferably at least thirty, and able to read. There's no overtime pay and the health benefits are pretty lousy, but it's a great way to get in shape before beach season.

32 elephants
10 elk
20 wild asses
10 tigers
40 wild horses
60 lions
30 leopards
10 hyenas
10 giraffes
6 hippos
1 rhinoceros
2,000 gladiators
several dozen ostriches

Given the massive Roman appetite for watching exotic animals get killed, it is worth mentioning that within a century of the Colosseum opening, most of the wild animals in Northern Africa are wiped out of existence.

If all this sounds delightful, the Romans wholeheartedly agree with you. They are often fanatically excited about these events. At a gladiator match in Pompeii in AD 59, fans of the local gladiators break out in a fight with fans from another city. The ensuing riot kills so many people that Pompeii is banned from holding gladiator matches for ten years. This is actually pretty tame compared to the Nika Riot in Constantinople in AD 532. The Nika Riot starts with a hotly contentious chariot race and ends five days later with thirty thousand dead and half the city burned down.

WHAT TO DO IF YOU ARE THROWN TO THE LIONS IN THE ROMAN COLOSSEUM

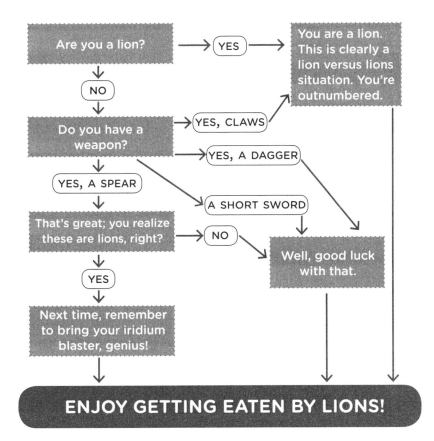

ENJOY GETTING EATEN BY LIONS!

Note: *Have you been fed to the lions? Are you looking for a good lawyer?* Cicero is Rome's top lawyer, and he insists we plug his legal services. No job is too small for Cicero, provided it offers him enormous publicity. Remember: Cicero may lose his head, but he will never lose your court case! Mention this ad and receive a 10 percent discount!

PRANKING THE PAST

Between your iridium blaster and your time machine, you have unlimited opportunities to prank the unsuspecting people of the past. If Rome's wild beast hunts seem a bit cruel to the animals, consider freeing the wild animals from the Colosseum and setting them loose in the streets of Rome. That might give the animals a fair shake.

Here's another way to level the playing field. Many gladiator matches pit weaponless prisoners against heavily armed soldiers. Time to even the score. Transport a platoon of US Marines armed with grenade launchers into the arena. See how it goes.

Preparing for Your Next Journey

If you're still alive at this point, you're probably getting the hang of ancient Rome. You know where to eat, where to shop, and how to avoid getting urine thrown on your head. You're now ready to tackle more dangerous and exciting adventures, like marching with the Roman army as it conquers Europe. To do this, you're going to need to meet one of the most powerful people in history. . . .

3
JULIUS CAESAR

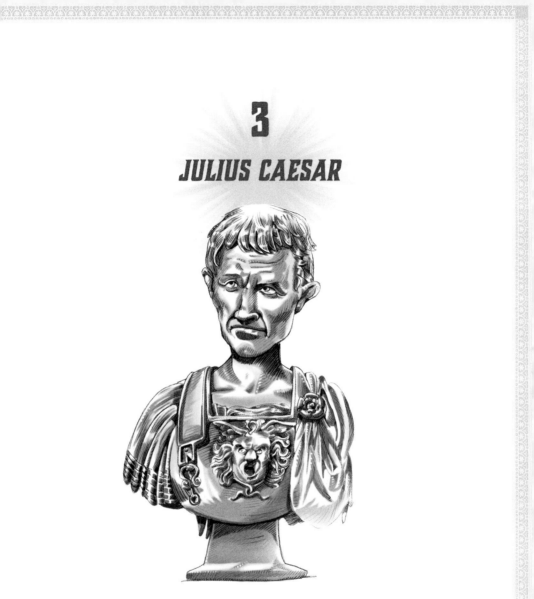

JULIUS CAESAR IS one of the greatest generals in history. He is also the first Roman dictator to rule the ancient world.* As part of Time Corp's thrilling vacation package to ancient Rome, you will get to experience Caesar's rise to power and witness the formation of one of the greatest empires the world has ever known,

---

*Finn Greenquill, corporate overlord of Time Corp, wishes us to mention that not *all* dictators are awful people. Julius Caesar is really not such a bad guy once you get to know him. Ask him anything about horses and he'll really open up.

besides Time Corp. In this chapter, we'll show you how to sign up with a Roman legion and march off to war with Caesar as he crushes all of Europe like a bug under his sandal.

Julius Caesar: The Early Years

If you want to get a feel for who Julius Caesar is, time jump to 75 BC, when Cilician pirates capture his ship.[*] The pirates hold twenty-five-year-old Caesar hostage on a Greek island and demand a ransom of twenty talents of gold (1,500 pounds of gold) to release him. Caesar finds this number insultingly low. He's worth far more than twenty talents of gold. He's so angry he promises the pirates he will crucify them. Caesar demands they raise their ransom demand to fifty talents (nearly 4,000 pounds of gold). The pirates have a good laugh at this, but they go along with it because, hey, free money.

Caesar's friends pay the hefty ransom. As soon as he's freed, Caesar commandeers a fleet and chases down the Cilician pirates on the high seas. He captures them, throws them in prison, and takes back his gold. The local governor wants to sell the pirates into slavery because it's far more profitable than just executing them. But Caesar, on his own authority, crucifies the pirates. A promise is a promise, and Caesar is a guy who keeps his word. However, as a sign of leniency to the pirates, he cuts their throats first.

....
*First, be sure to purchase one of Time Corp's very affordable life insurance policies.

HELPFUL HINTS: ROMAN SCHOOL

Caesar, like all Roman students, is required to learn reading, writing, arithmetic, speech, and weaponry. Roman school classes begin at dawn. There are no schoolhouses, so school is held anywhere—a park, street corner, or even the teacher's apartment. The teacher sits on a sort of throne while the students sit on benches.

There are no weekends, but school is let out for some holidays. Summer vacation lasts from June until mid-October. Students are taught through a delightful cocktail of grueling memorization and violent beatings. Even though many teachers are slaves, they can still beat their students.

Here are some actual Roman teaching methods:

1. Twist the student's ear. That should help him learn.
2. If that doesn't work, hold the student's hands against a flat piece of wood and beat his knuckles with a reed cane.
3. If the student still isn't learning, the teacher may beat the student with a leather whip.
4. Still not learning? The student may be stripped naked and laid across the backs of two other

students. One holds down the student's arms, the other the legs. The student is then beaten mercilessly with a wooden stick.[*]

School is completed by age thirteen or fourteen. There is no high school or college. But if a student wants to continue on with literature, public speaking, or being beaten, they can continue to employ a special tutor.

Marching to War with Caesar

Julius Caesar rapidly scales the political ladder, rising through the ranks, until he's finally elected consul. A consul is roughly equivalent to a modern president, except you get to command your very own personal army. Up until this point, Julius Caesar is a good politician, writer, orator, soldier, and horseman. But he's about to become one of the greatest military leaders of all time. So snag yourself a Roman army uniform and set your Time Corp Time Machine SE™ to 56 BC, because it's time for . . .

Caesar's Conquest of Europe

Caesar, starting with only two legions (about ten thousand soldiers),

---

[*]Romans have a particular respect for creative punishments. By Roman law, if a child kills their father, the punishment is to be tied up in a sack with a rooster, a snake, a dog, and a monkey, and thrown into the ocean.

proceeds to take over Europe, ballooning the size of Roman territory. What follows are some high points you may want to witness.

First off, if you want to blend into Caesar's army, Time Corp can get you a good deal on a legionary's uniform and kit.

THE ROMAN LEGIONARY

Most of these items are from so far in the past,
Time Corp is not even sure what they're for.

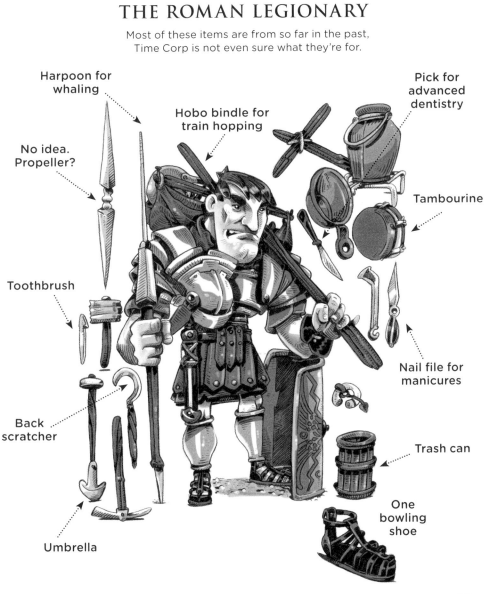

Harpoon for whaling

Hobo bindle for train hopping

Pick for advanced dentistry

No idea. Propeller?

Tambourine

Toothbrush

Nail file for manicures

Back scratcher

Trash can

One bowling shoe

Umbrella

Life as a Roman soldier has its perks: cool weapons, cool plunder, international travel . . . But if you are considering a career in the Roman army, keep in mind a legionary is paid only nine hundred sesterces per year, with half deducted for food and living expenses. If you're lucky enough to get paid, you're looking at a whopping one and a half sesterces per day. Barely enough to buy a loaf of bread and a drink. Put another way, a donkey costs five hundred sesterces, which is more money than you'll save in a year. If you're a common Roman soldier, you are worth less than a donkey.

Barbarians

If you are going to join a Roman legion, like it or not, you're probably going to fight some barbarians. Who are the barbarians, you ask? Anyone in Europe who does not have the good fortune to be a Roman is a barbarian. They may be German, French, Spanish, Swedish—doesn't matter. Basically, angry folks who don't like Romans and have gone their whole lives without a shower. These are the guys Caesar wants to conquer.

WHAT TO DO IF YOU ARE ATTACKED BY A BARBARIAN

1. Don't panic. The barbarian is probably as afraid of you as you are of it.

2. Spread your arms to appear as large as possible.

3. The barbarian's most effective weapon is his bow. Also his sword. And spear. And ax. And cudgel. And his bare hands and yellow teeth. But don't worry: you're from the future! Disable his weapons using your iridium blaster.

4. Try to knock the barbarian from his horse[*] to limit his mobility.

5. The barbarian fights with metal weapons. They cannot penetrate your iridium shielding, so you can simply walk away at this point, if necessary.

6. Do not feed the barbarian. He may follow you for hundreds of miles.

7. If you experience any trouble with steps 1 through 6, simply start over using your nuclear chronometer.

Women in Caesar's Army

If you are female, there are several ways to blend into Caesar's army. The easiest might be to dress as a legionary. Roman soldiers crop their hair very short. So if you have long hair, just tie it up and remember to never, ever take off your helmet.

Plenty of women march with Caesar's army, often as cooks and seamstresses.[†] The soldiers are also allowed to live with their wives while deployed on the front lines. Caesar's successor, Augustus, will eventually ban soldiers from getting married.

....

[*]Horse: the barbarian's mobility device. Think of it as a sort of nonfloating hover-car that runs on hay instead of fission. For those with short-term memory problems, see "Helpful Hints" on page 16, entitled "How to Pilot a Horse." Then, for those with especially bad short-term memory problems, remember to turn back to this section.

[†]Women are not allowed to be soldiers in ancient Rome. But they are allowed to be most other skilled professions, including scribes, merchants, actresses, import dealers, innkeepers, barmaids, and doctors.

This may be because of a massive Roman defeat at the Battle of the Teutoburg Forest. When the Germans attack, the Roman soldiers rush to rescue their wives instead of fighting. Twenty thousand Romans are massacred that day.

If You Need to See a Doctor

Traveling to foreign countries to slaughter barbarians is hard work. If you get sick or injured in the Roman Empire, one of the most dangerous things you can possibly do is see a doctor.

If you are marching with a Roman legion, every army camp has a *medicus*. This person is a professional combat medic, surgeon, and often a veterinarian,* taking care of the horses. Roman medics see a tremendous amount of combat injuries, and are actually pretty good at setting broken bones and sewing up stab wounds. They're well equipped with scalpels, forceps, catheters, and bone saws, and can even use opium, henbane, and mandrake to numb pain during surgery.

Where Roman doctors fall a bit short is in treating any form of illness whatsoever.

To be fair, Roman doctors are the best in the ancient world. They wash their hands before surgery, have a fair understanding of

....

*Finn Greenquill insists we point out that a veterinarian who has served in the military is a vet vet. And if that veterinarian does not eat meat, then they are a vegetarian veterinarian veteran. Every day, Mr. Greenquill continues to dazzle us with his insight. This is why it is such a pleasure to work at Time Corp 14 hours a day, with only a half hour for lunch and no coffee breaks.

malaria, and invent a staggering number of the terms used in modern medicine. Still, without microscopes or a germ theory of disease, Roman doctors are often just going on guesswork. Some pills prescribed simply contain dried bugs. For many ailments, Cato the Elder—a noted statesman—recommends cabbage.

HELPFUL HINTS: ASK A ROMAN DOCTOR

Here are actual medical recommendations recorded from noted Roman doctors.

Bit by a rabid dog? Get a piece of dried hyena skin. Put it on the wound. See how that works.

Snake bite? Pour wine up your nose and smear the snake bite in pig excrement.

Fever? Your problem is you have too much blood. We can fix that. We'll just open up a vein to drain your extra blood. Or use leeches to suck it out of you. Not complaining about that fever now, are you?

Epilepsy? No problem. Drink the blood of a fallen gladiator.

Jaundice? Simple. Spike a glass of wine with the

ashes of a deer antler and the blood of a donkey.

Sleepy? No worries. Take a donkey's calluses, soak them in vinegar, and cram them up your nostrils. Awake now?

Off to War

Spoiler alert: Caesar beats *everyone*. In eight years' time, Caesar conquers roughly 135,000 square miles of Europe. He slaughters nearly one million French people, enslaves another million, subdues more than three hundred tribes, and razes about eight hundred towns. And what have *you* accomplished lately?

ALL THE LAND CAESAR CONQUERS IN EUROPE, 58-51 BC

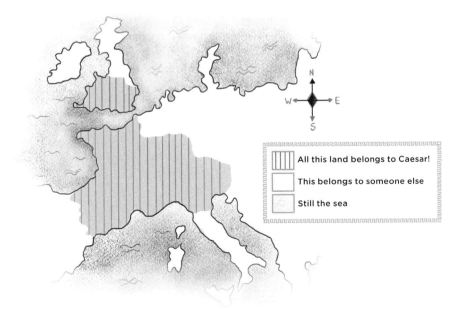

N
W E
S

All this land belongs to Caesar!

This belongs to someone else

Still the sea

Caesar Beats the Swiss, Belgians, Germans, and British

If you're going to march with Caesar's army, just know that it gets a bit on the bloody side. You may want to bring a fresh change of clothes, or even just wear red. Of the 370,000 Swiss tribal people, Caesar slaughters 200,000. To be fair, the Swiss technically started it.

The Germans decide to start raiding Caesar's French allies, so Caesar crosses the Rhine River into Germany and crushes every settlement he encounters. Twice. Next, the Belgians pick a fight with Caesar, so he takes over their country. Caesar becomes the first Roman to enter Britain, and conquers their country, too, for good measure. The moral? *You do not mess with Caesar.*

PRANKING THE PAST: BATTLE ROULETTE

Ever wonder who would win a fight, a Roman legionary or a samurai? Time to find out. Simply travel to feudal Japan, find an unsuspecting flock of samurai, and transport them inside a Roman army barracks.

NOTE: While our legal team does not officially condone gambling, betting can be done through Time Corp's bookies on Soltarian 7.

Caesar Just Absolutely Destroys the French

Strap on your bronze armor and set your time machine for 52 BC. A young French chief named Vercingetorix[*] still hasn't learned the lesson: *you do not mess with Caesar.* Vercingetorix raises an army of Frenchmen and incites them to revolt. He attempts to starve the Romans out of France by destroying every farm his army comes across. Vercingetorix hates Romans so much, he's literally burning down France to get rid of them.[†]

To feed his rebel forces, Vercingetorix spares only one town in the countryside: Avaricum. Their farms are left unburned. Caesar's hungry army now has exactly one choice: conquer Avaricum.

By the time Caesar's legions arrive, they're outnumbered and starved half to death. But they do have one asset: Julius Caesar. The Romans crush Avaricum into sawdust, put all its inhabitants to the sword, and collect nearly all the remaining food in France. Now well fed, the Roman army is ready to obliterate Vercingetorix.[‡]

Vercingetorix flees to the French town of Alesia. You can ride in pursuit with Caesar's army. Or, if you're not good on a horse, you can always just time jump there. Caesar besieges the town,

....

[*]If you have trouble pronouncing this name, so do we. Imagine if your parents were cruel enough to name you Vercingetorix. You'd probably grow up to be an angry warlord, too.

[†]Vercingetorix is a really fun word to write. Vercingetorix, Vercingetorix, Vercingetorix.

[‡]Vercingetorix, Vercingetorix, Vercingetorix, Vercingetorix, Vercingetorix. Vercingetorix.

surrounding 80,000 French with only 60,000 Romans. Things get even trickier for Caesar on October 2, 52 BC, when *250,000* fresh French troops arrive and besiege Caesar.* Caesar is now the Roman jelly inside a really big French doughnut.

SIEGE OF ALESIA

Caesar's Roman forces

Vercingetorix's Gallic forces

Caesar's Roman fortifications

French backup forces

Caesar is completely surrounded and wildly outnumbered. If you are with Caesar's army at this point, you may want to consider switching sides. Or you can try one of Time Corp's safer vacation packages. Maybe visit some beaches in Hawaii a few centuries before all the tourists arrive?

If you're sure you want to stay, and you've signed all of Time

---

*Caesar puts the number at 250,000. The Roman historian Plutarch estimates 300,000. Both numbers may be exaggerated. We've traveled to the battle and tried counting the French, but they won't keep still.

Corp's legal waivers, then sharpen your sword and your wits. This is a vicious fight. The French armies mercilessly attack Caesar from both sides, with overwhelming numbers. This should be very bad news for Caesar, except for one important fact that should be abundantly clear by now: YOU DO NOT MESS WITH CAESAR.

HELPFUL HINTS: TIME CORP DELIVERY SERVICE

If you are in the middle of a Roman battle, and find yourself in need of a weapon, or simply some refreshment, just dial *1-800-THRIFTY* and a messenger will deliver anything your heart desires. We offer maces, cudgels, and pickaxes at affordable prices. If you are really in a bind and see no way of winning the battle fairly, you can always just rent an iridium blaster. A messenger will arrive at your battlefield to get your credit card information and deliver your package. Don't forget to tip your messenger; they are risking life and limb to provide you with excellent service.

Caesar's troops hold their defensive line as a sea of Frenchmen attack from both sides. The Romans do not break. Meanwhile, Caesar does something so crazy it should never work in a million years.* *He attacks.* Though completely outnumbered, he smashes his way through the French line and circles around to attack their rear. With only six thousand cavalry, Caesar attacks sixty thousand French. This shocks everyone, including the Romans. Caesar's legions are so astonished by his bravery, they fight twice as hard. The French army turns in confusion and panic. They break and run. The Romans slaughter as many as ninety thousand French. Caesar claims his men would have butchered all the French, but their sword arms simply became too exhausted from all the hacking. Vercingetorix surrenders and will spend the next five years in a Roman prison before being strangled.

Crossing the Rubicon

Julius Caesar, now the most powerful man in Roman history, starts out toward home to take a victory lap. His fame and power worry the nervous nobility in the Roman Senate. The Senate votes to deny Caesar his right to a victory parade and orders him to disband his army and return to Rome alone and unarmed. There's gratitude for you. Caesar just about doubles the size of the Roman Empire and this is the thanks he gets!

Caesar just spent ten years conquering Europe and does not want to disband his loyal army. Not content with beating every country in Europe, Caesar now sets his sights on the one country

....
*This literally never works in a million years. We have a time machine: we've checked.

he hasn't beaten: his own. On January 10, 49 BC, Caesar utters this immortal words *"Iacta alea est"*—"the die is cast" —when he defies the Senate's orders by crossing the Rubicon River back into Italy . . . *with his army.*

Are You Still Alive?

If you have not yet been gutted by a barbarian, you have our sincere congratulations. You can always rush home to the future—no one will judge you for it. But if you really want to get your money's worth, march with Caesar as he goes on to conquer the world. . . .

4

THE ROMAN CIVIL WAR

WITH CAESAR MARCHING on Rome at the head of his army, the Senate panics.* Desperate for protection, they grant General Pompey control over all of Rome's remaining armies. This leads to an epic showdown between the two greatest generals in the Republic.

Pompey used to be Caesar's closest ally. He helped get Caesar elected to consul, with help from Crassus—the richest man in Rome. But it may be worth noting that Caesar secretly dated one of Pompey's wives, Mucia. When Pompey found out, he divorced her. While we're at it, we should probably mention that Caesar also secretly dated Crassus's wife, Tertulla.

To make things even more complicated, Pompey was also married to Julius Caesar's daughter, Julia. This meant that Pompey was Caesar's son-in-law, even though Pompey was older than Caesar. Imagine a Thanksgiving dinner at Caesar's house . . . Awkward.

....

*If you're interested in entering Roman politics, just know that you must have a net worth of at least one million sesterces to be allowed to run for the Senate!

HELPFUL HINTS: ROMAN MARRIAGE

If you find someone you want to marry in ancient Rome, congratulations. Here are a few pointers on Roman marriage. In Rome, boys are considered ready for marriage by age fourteen, and girls are considered ready by age twelve. If a girl makes it all the way to age twenty without getting hitched, it's considered abnormal. In fact, Caesar's successor, Emperor Augustus, makes women over age twenty pay severe fines if they stay single. Single men are fined after age twenty-five. There are also several laws governing which marriages are legal for Roman citizens:

WHOM YOU ARE ALLOWED TO MARRY IN ANCIENT ROME

Your uncle	Sure
Your niece	Why not?
A foreigner	Nope
A slave	No way
A former slave	Sorry
A soldier	Gross
Your cousin	Totally
Your aunt	Good idea
A twelve-year-old	Of course!

If you decide to get married in ancient Rome, it's worth knowing that the man can do pretty much whatever he wants. It's legal for the man of the house to sell his wife and children into slavery. If the mood strikes him, he can even put his own children to death. He can also command his children to get married, or, if he changes his mind, command them to get divorced. If he isn't satisfied with the quality of a newborn baby, he can order it to be abandoned. So if you're going to marry a Roman, if at all possible, try to be male.*

Pompey the Great

The Senate commands Pompey to destroy Caesar's army. This war is not to be missed. Caesar is a great general, but "Pompey the Great" is no slouch. Pompey commanded his first army at age

*As tricky as it is to get married in Rome, it's amazingly easy to get divorced. One has simply to declare, in public, that you are now divorced. That's it. No lawyers, no fuss.

twenty-three and fought campaigns in Sicily, Africa, Spain, and Italy. After successfully defeating most of the pirates in the Mediterranean, he expanded Roman territory in Turkey, Syria, and Greece. Pompey is credited with conquering over 1,000 forts, 900 cities, 800 pirate ships, as well as founding 39 new cities.

Caesar's army quickly occupies Rome. Pompey, caught totally unprepared, flees. He takes a fast boat to Greece, where he rallies his troops.

The good news is, Caesar now controls Italy. The bad news is, Caesar is in the middle of a Pompey sandwich. Pompey commands an army in Greece, and Pompey's lieutenants command the Roman army in Spain. Taking things one step at a time, Caesar crosses the Pyrenees Mountains into Spain. A siege here, a siege there, and Caesar crushes his opposition.

A DELICIOUS POMPEY SANDWICH, WITH A SIDE OF CAESAR

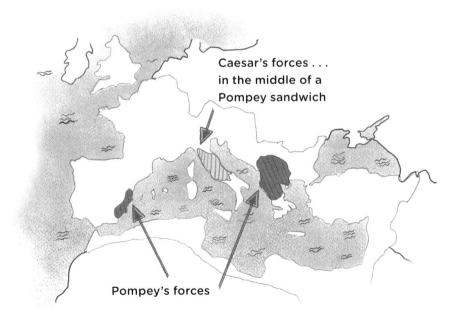

Caesar's forces . . . in the middle of a Pompey sandwich

Pompey's forces

Next, Caesar returns to Italy and attempts to sail to Greece to attack Pompey. But he has one problem: a man named Bibulus.

A few years earlier, Bibulus made the mistake of blocking one of Caesar's Senate bills. This error ended with an angry mob dragging Bibulus out of the Senate and dumping a barrel of excrement on him. Bibulus was so humiliated he didn't leave his house for a year. Bibulus now hates Caesar with every fiber of his being. It is the great passion of his life. And Bibulus controls the Roman navy.

Bibulus attempts to trap Caesar's army by blockading the Italian docks, but Caesar's ships sneak past him and successfully cross to Greece. Bibulus, hopping mad, decides to blockade *the entire Adriatic Sea*. This will prevent Caesar from getting any more food, weapons, or troops from Italy. Bibulus's plan is to starve Caesar out of Greece. But Bibulus is forgetting one crucial lesson: You Do Not Mess with Caesar.

Some of Caesar's soldiers are in Greece and some are still stuck in Italy. So Caesar pulls off a military feat that has never been equaled in history: he beats a naval blockade with a land blockade. Caesar lines the coasts of Greece *and* Italy with his own soldiers to prevent Bibulus's navy from landing to gather fresh water or food. With nowhere to safely land ships, Bibulus's crews slowly die of hunger and thirst. Bibulus himself dies of exposure within a few weeks. Without the use of a single warship, Caesar beats the Roman navy.

Safely cross the Adriatic Sea with Caesar's army, and you can watch him battle Pompey at the Battle of Dyrrachium on July 10, 48 BC. This is an interesting battle to witness, because it's one

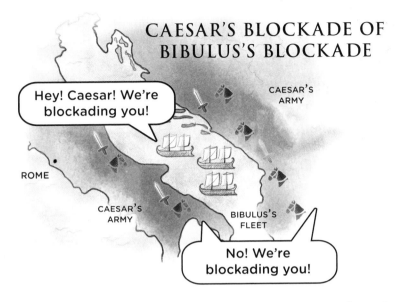

of the few Caesar doesn't win. Pompey's army outnumbers Caesar's three to one, and Caesar cannot gain any advantage. Caesar retreats inland to the Greek town of Pharsalus in order to draw Pompey away from his supplies on the coast. . . .

Battle of Pharsalus

Set your Time Corp Time Machine SE™ to August 9, 48 BC, and join in one of the most astonishing victories in military history. Pompey and Caesar square off for battle. Pompey has every tactical advantage: he commands the high ground, he has better supplies, and his army is more than twice as large as Caesar's. Yet Caesar outmaneuvers Pompey completely, using his 22,000 men to defeat an army of 45,000. At battle's end, Caesar claims to have lost only 230 men, while Pompey may have lost as many as 15,000. Pompey throws off his general's cloak, grabs his wife and his stash of gold, and flees to Egypt.

Welcome to Egypt, Pompey

Pompey, on the run, begs the Egyptians for a place to hide. Pompey is old friends with the Egyptians, having done them a few handy favors, like conquering all of the pirates in the Mediterranean. The thirteen-year-old Egyptian pharaoh, Ptolemy XIII, meets with his counselors to decide whether to harbor Pompey. They know Caesar's on his way with a gigantic army. So they decide it's safer to side with Caesar. . . .

Ptolemy lures Pompey to the Egyptian shore, sending a ship to give him a lift. The young pharaoh sets up his throne on the dock and watches his men row Pompey to shore. At the arranged moment, Ptolemy's men stab Pompey to death and decapitate him. When Caesar arrives in Egypt, Ptolemy offers him a cheerful welcome gift: Pompey's severed head.

HELPFUL HINTS:
MAYBE DON'T GET BEHEADED

Keeping your head in the past is no easy matter. Time travel is tricky business. From the Aztec temples to the French Revolution, people will constantly be trying to separate you from your head.

Few things can make a bad day worse than being decapitated. And keep in mind, your beheading creates enormous headaches for the good people at Time Corp. Nothing makes an insurance company grind their teeth more than a customer dying before they were born.

Think of the grave-cutter writing: "Here lies [Your Name], Born AD 2150, Died AD 445. Killed by Attila the Hun over a poker match." Think of your grandchildren battling over your will with your great-great-grandparents. In a word: awkward. So if you're going to spend time with Egyptians, Greeks, Persians, or other people with a hankering for beheading, tip generously and laugh at all of their jokes.

One more helpful tip: if you're thinking of starting a violent palace coup, toppling a government, or launching a civil war, maybe don't. Couldn't hurt.

PEOPLE TO HAVE LUNCH WITH:
CRASSUS

Crassus is the richest man in Rome and one of the richest men of all time . . . though not quite as rich as the handsome, talented, and inspiring CEO of Time Corp, Finn Greenquill. The Roman author Pliny the Elder estimates Crassus's fortune to be 200 million sesterces. This is more money than the entire Roman treasury, so in a sense, Crassus is richer than Rome. Whatever the case, when you're having lunch with Crassus, don't reach for the bill when the check arrives.

When Crassus was a young man, his political ene-mies exiled him and seized all of his family's money. Crassus became penniless. After years in exile, Cras-sus was able to return to Rome and get a job working for his friend Sulla, who happened to be the consul of Rome (basically, the president). Crassus never wanted to be poor again. He proceeded to get fantas-tically rich in five ways:

1. **Stealing from dead people.** Crassus used his government post to seize the property of ex-ecuted criminals. In his efforts to rebuild his fortunes, there is decent evidence Crassus some-times executed innocent men just to get his hands on valuable estates.

2. **Slave trading.** Very lucrative business. Greek slaves are highly educated. French and German slaves are strong and hardworking. Child slaves are much cheaper, though less reliable.... But hey, you get what you pay for.

3. **Extorting real estate.** Rome has fires every night, but no fire department. So Crassus trains five hundred of his slaves to form a fire brigade. Each night, Crassus rushes his slaves to a burn-ing house and offers to buy it. The distressed homeowner then sells his burning house for any price, literally at fire-sale prices. Crassus's slaves

then extinguish the fire. In this way, Crassus buys up entire neighborhoods of Rome.

4. **Silver mines.** Always a good investment when you can literally dig money out of the ground.

5. **Rent-a-Slave.** Crassus rents out his slaves by the hour, the day, the week, or even the year.

Remember Spartacus, the Thracian gladiator who leads the slave revolt in 73 BC? Well, slaves are a great passion of Crassus's, so he raises two legions at his own expense and goes to war with Spartacus. The first time Crassus's army faces Spartacus, his men throw down their weapons and flee. Crassus punishes his men with decimation, killing one-tenth of his own army. This does much to inspire the fighting spirit of his troops, who now realize Crassus is more dangerous to them than the enemy. They go on to defeat Spartacus.

Not content to be the richest man in the world, Crassus longs for military victories to rival those of Caesar and Pompey. Once he gains the post of Governor of Syria in 53 BC, Crassus leads a Roman invasion of Iran. It turns out Crassus is better at making money than leading soldiers. The Iranian horse archers utterly defeat Crassus's heavy infantry at the Battle of Carrhae. Of Crassus's 40,000 troops, 10,000 are captured and 20,000 are killed. After assassinating Crassus, the Iranians pour molten gold into his mouth as a symbol of his thirst for wealth.

HELPFUL HINTS:
WHAT TO DO IF YOU
ARE ENSLAVED IN ROME

The refreshing thing about slavery in Rome is that *anyone* can become a slave. Even if you're a Roman. Many slaves are people conquered by the Roman army, such as Greeks, French, Germans, British, Syrians, or Carthaginians. Other slaves are simply abandoned children who are rounded up on the streets.

Slaves are often well educated. Some are doctors, teachers, accountants, scribes, and architects. The menial work in Rome is often done by free poor people rather than by the more expensive slaves. There are as many as three million slaves in the Roman Empire in Caesar's day, at least 35 percent of the population.

If you do become enslaved, don't lose hope. It is fairly common to be released from slavery, or to buy your way out. Freed slaves often become extremely rich, because they know more about business than the aristocrats. In fact, some of the wealthiest people in Rome are former slaves.

CRASSUS'S RENT-A-SLAVE

> **Service:** ★
> **Accepts Credit Cards:** No ✕
> **Cost:** $ $ $ $
> **Danger of Revolt:** High

Slaves are some of the most highly educated people in Rome. After Rome conquers Greece, Italy is flooded with mathematicians, philosophers, engineers, architects, and artists. These slaves make for useful tutors because of their command of foreign languages. There's really no better way to teach your daughter French than to purchase her a teacher captured in France.

★★ "I hired a Greek interpreter. He spoke seven languages. But not English. I tried to ask Crassus for my money back, and he had me flogged by a centurion."

—Bob R., Wallingford, CT

★★★ "I hired a gladiator slave, and he beat me with a sickle. My insurance doesn't cover this. I'm only giving this company three stars."

—Sally S., Rockford, IL

★ "Crassus had me sign a legal agreement when I rented my slave. I don't read Latin, so I had no idea I was signing away my freedom. Now I'm a slave in one of Crassus's silver mines in Spain. I would not recommend Crassus's Rent-a-Slave to a friend."

—Alex M., Crested Butte, CO

Hi everyone!

Finn Greenquill here, CEO of Time Corp. I'm currently dictating this speech to my assistant, Clarence, as we race across the tropical seas of the Jurassic period on my hover-yacht. Clarence is a genetically engineered, hyperintelligent dire wolf, spawned in 2161. He is a mediocre pilot at best, at least while he's taking dictation, but he mixes a mean Arnold Palmer.

Time Corp employees are constantly coming up to me and saying things like, "Finn, please tell us more about yourself and how wonderful you are," or, "Mr. Greenquill, please tell us how you built the monolithic bureaucracy of Time Corp which now encompasses all sixty-three moons of Jupiter," or, "Mr. Greenquill, we haven't had a day off in fifteen years; may we please get a fifteen-minute coffee break to celebrate Christmas?"

To these I say, "Absolutely," "With pleasure," and "Not on your life."

Time Corp graced the world shortly after I discovered the solution to time travel. The solution to time travel, as it happens, was sitting on the desk of my college roommate, an egghead physicist named Clarence. I did not give Clarence any shares in my future company, but I did name my favorite dire wolf after him. After ripping off Clarence's plans, I gave his design schematics to an engineer in my dorm, who then built the first time machine out of a lava lamp and a used Honda Civic.

To raise the money to launch Time Corp, I traveled back in time and made some very well-informed bets on the 1927 Yankees. I then invested the winnings in New York real estate. By the time I returned to the present day, I was wealthy beyond my wildest dreams, or at least wealthy enough to field Clarence's legal claims. For management advice on launching Time Corp, I befriended myself in the future, to find out exactly how I turned Time Corp into such a roaring success.

By this point, you're probably thinking two things: "Isn't changing history illegal?" and "How does Clarence the dire wolf pilot a hover-yacht with only his paws?"

First of all, yes, the Time Patrol ensures that it is completely illegal for anyone besides me to permanently change history. "But that's not fair!" you say. Well, if you donate forty quadrillion dollars to the annual Police Charity Golf Tournament, you can get a free pass, too.

As for Clarence's piloting skills, all I can tell you is

that he is extremely intelligent and there is very little for us to crash into in the middle of the Jurassic ocean. But I digress.

On behalf of myself and my quadrillions of dollars, I'd like to personally thank each and every one of you for buying my guidebook. Your expensive travels to the past are helping to make my financial future ever brighter.

Thank you all most affectionately,

Finn Greenquill

Founder and Corporate Overlord, Time Corp

5

QUALITY TIME WITH CLEOPATRA

WHEN MAMMOTHS STILL roamed the earth, the Egyptian civilization was already centuries old. Here in Caesar's day, the Sphinx is already so old it is invisible, buried under the sands. The Great Pyramids are about 35 feet taller than in modern times, not yet worn down by millennia of erosion.

Caesar's just spent four years fighting the Roman civil war. So he's less than thrilled to arrive in Egypt just in time for . . . you guessed it . . . *another* civil war. You remember that Ptolemy XIII rules Egypt, but he shares the throne with his big sister, *and wife,* Cleopatra VII. It's common for Egyptian pharaohs to marry their siblings in order to keep power within one family. Suffice it to say, Ptolemy and Cleopatra each want Egypt for themselves. Caesar is the most powerful man in the world, so whichever sibling can make friends with Caesar will rule Egypt.

Naturally, Cleopatra wants to make a good first impression on Caesar. But what do you get for the man who has everything? Her brother Ptolemy already gave Caesar Pompey's decapitated head. Cleo needs to go the extra mile.

To get a private audience with Caesar, she does what any sensible person would do. She wraps herself in a carpet, and her servants deliver her to Caesar's chambers.[*] Once alone with Caesar, she rolls herself out of the carpet and casually introduces herself. Very suave. If you choose to sneak into Caesar's chambers, it's worth watching this just for the expression on his face.

Cleopatra is only twenty-one, but Roman historians agree she is already one of the cleverest people in the world. One of the perks of living in the city of Alexandria is that it contains the Library of Alexandria, the center of learning in the ancient world. This means the greatest scholars on earth are Cleopatra's teachers. Weekends haven't been invented yet, so growing up, Cleopatra spends every day of her life studying, except for occasional holidays. She speaks nine languages. She is Greek; her family has ruled Egypt for generations. She's the first member of

---

*You can enter the chambers using your iridium blaster, but try to be subtle about it.

her family to actually bother to learn Egyptian, so she can command her army without interpreters. Most importantly, she's received an enormous amount of training in public speaking, persuasion, and charm. Her sparkling eyes, keen wit, and ability to flatter her audience have been trained into her by her tutors for years. This is who Caesar is up against when Cleopatra sneaks into his chambers. She presents her case for why Caesar should side with her in a war against her brother.

Besides her wit and charm, Cleopatra gives Caesar plenty of reasons to like her. Not only is she the richest person in the world—even richer than Crassus—but she is a direct descendant of Alexander the Great's general, Ptolemy I. Caesar worships Alexander the Great, an ancient Greek who conquered the world by age thirty-three. Once, while gazing at a statue of Alexander, Caesar abruptly bursts into tears, ashamed of how little he's accomplished when compared to Alexander.

The bottom line is Caesar needs gobs of money to keep paying his army, and Cleopatra keeps making gobs of money because she owns Egypt. What Cleopatra really needs is Caesar's army to support her claims on the Egyptian throne. So they decide to scratch each other's backs. It's a match made in heaven.

When thirteen-year-old Ptolemy XIII finds out his big sister met with Caesar, he bursts into tears, runs out into the street, and throws an epic temper tantrum. He then raises his army and attempts to fight Caesar. Big mistake. Caesar helps Cleopatra win the civil war. Young Ptolemy XIII drowns while fleeing across the Nile River.

The City of Alexandria

When you enter Alexandria, the capital of Egypt, you will be daz-
zled by the gleaming white marble buildings. The main street is
100 feet wide, large enough for eight chariots to ride abreast. The
famous 450-foot lighthouse is one of the Seven Wonders of the
World.

At night, the city is lit with lamps and torchlight. Thirty-foot
statues of sphinxes line the city square, alongside three-story-
high statues of the Ptolemaic kings and queens. Every plinth and
archway in the city is adorned with stone sculptures of animal
gods.

By day, the streets are crammed with Libyan merchants, Judean soldiers, Greek scholars, purple-cloaked Egyptian court officials, and camel caravans bearing silk from Sheba. The wealth of the Nile flows through Alexandria's bustling ports. The city even boasts a zoo with giraffes, cheetahs, and lions. Alexandria is the most beautiful city of its time. In fact, you really should have purchased our Alexandria time travel package rather than Rome. Well, live and learn.

HELPFUL HINTS: TOURISM

Romans are avid tourists. They travel to Athens to visit the house where Socrates once lived, they travel to see the Seven Wonders of the World, and they travel to watch the Olympics. People throughout the ancient world will not find it at all odd that you are a tourist, though they may be confused by your camera and cargo shorts.

A Greek traveler named Pausanias writes what may be the first travel guide in history. It's published in the second century AD, and features ten books, each focusing on a different area of Greece. The guide points out notable historical landmarks and local wildlife, and mentions local folklore.[*]

*While it's true Pausanias wrote a pretty good travel guide, Finn Greenquill insists that *The Thrifty Guide to Ancient Greece* is clearly the superior guidebook for today's savvy traveler. Frankly, Pausanias is now dead and doesn't need the royalties, whereas Finn Greenquill has several mortgages on luxury hover-yachts that simply aren't going to pay for themselves.

Pleasure Cruise up the Nile

Caesar and Cleopatra begin dating, even though he is now fifty-two and she is only twenty-one. And even though he's still married to his third wife and she's recently widowed from her own murdered brother. But hey, nobody's perfect.

Caesar wins the Egyptian civil war for Cleopatra, which is a pretty big favor. So Cleopatra takes him on a pleasure cruise up the Nile, stopping at all the major sights. If you can score an invitation to this boat ride, we highly recommend it. The meals are ridiculously pricey—you may enjoy the roasted pig served on a gold platter and stuffed with thrushes. Slaves drop rose petals continuously throughout each meal; some 300 pounds' worth are required every feast. Visiting dinner guests are sent home with lavish gifts. After a typical dinner, Cleopatra may send you home with a silver place setting, a silver sofa, a slave, a gazelle, and a gold-armored horse.

Before long, Caesar and Cleopatra have a son named Caesarion, or "Little Caesar." The two biggest celebrities in the ancient world having a child together causes a huge tabloid sensation. Surely, it seems, Caesarion will inherit the whole world.

Cleopatra's Family

Some of you may be disturbed by the idea of Cleopatra marrying her own brother and then going to war with him. But the truth of

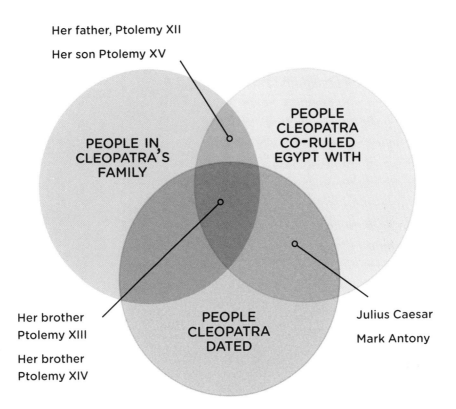

Her father, Ptolemy XII

Her son Ptolemy XV

PEOPLE IN CLEOPATRA'S FAMILY

PEOPLE CLEOPATRA CO-RULED EGYPT WITH

Her brother Ptolemy XIII

Her brother Ptolemy XIV

PEOPLE CLEOPATRA DATED

Julius Caesar

Mark Antony

the matter is, in Cleopatra's family, this is a time-honored tradition.

Royal blood is considered sacred, so it's common in Cleopatra's family to marry family members in order to keep the bloodline pure. Of course, upon ascending the throne, murdering off siblings and rivals is really the logical thing to do. Cleopatra dutifully follows in her family's footsteps, and will eventually kill all four of her siblings. Puts new meaning to the phrase "sibling rivalry."

Cleopatra's parents are cousins, and her grandparents are brothers and sisters. This means she only has one set of great-grandparents, instead of four. Cleopatra doesn't have a family tree so much as a family stump. Suffice it to say, she has fewer gifts to buy on holidays.

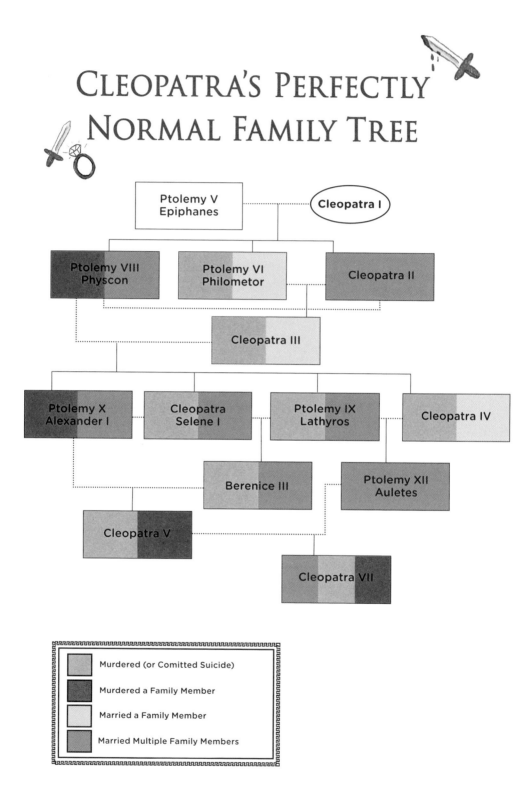

CLEOPATRA'S PERFECTLY NORMAL FAMILY TREE

Ptolemy V Epiphanes

Cleopatra I

Ptolemy VIII Physcon

Ptolemy VI Philometor

Cleopatra II

Cleopatra III

Ptolemy X Alexander I

Cleopatra Selene I

Ptolemy IX Lathyros

Cleopatra IV

Berenice III

Ptolemy XII Auletes

Cleopatra V

Cleopatra VII

Murdered (or Comitted Suicide)

Murdered a Family Member

Married a Family Member

Married Multiple Family Members

A Few Quick Notes on Cleopatra's Perfectly Normal Family Tree

1. Yes, all the men in Cleopatra's family are named Ptolemy. Makes family reunions very confusing. But at least they get bulk rates on their monogrammed bath towels.

2. Ptolemy IV murders his mother, who killed his father, who was dating his grandmother. He then marries his sister Arsinoë III, who is later murdered by the palace staff.

3. Ptolemy XI murders his wife after only nineteen days of marriage. He is immediately killed by an angry mob.

4. Ptolemy VIII starts a civil war with his wife, Cleopatra II, by marrying her daughter, Cleopatra III. He then kills his son and mails the body parts to Cleopatra II for her birthday. She makes the unusual choice of displaying the body parts in public. A few years later, *they reconcile.* Ptolemy—married to both his niece and his sister—rules with two queens.* Gotta love happy endings.

*Time Corp's legal department, wishing to avoid any lawsuits from ancient Egyptians, would like to point out that this is *all true*. Seriously.

HELPFUL HINTS: UNDERSTANDING CLEOPATRA'S FAMILY TREE

Cleopatra's family tree may be a tiny bit confusing, so let's make this as clear as possible.

Ptolemy VIII married Cleopatra II, who was also his sister. She had a daughter, Cleopatra III, whom he married as well. So his stepdaughter was his wife and his niece, and his wife was his sister and his mother-in-law, because she was the mother of his wife. Easy, right?

This made Ptolemy his own father-in-law, because he is the husband of his wife's mother. Simple.

It's very straightforward. If you are Cleopatra III, then your husband is your uncle and your mother is your aunt, because she is your uncle's sister.

We're not sure how to make this any simpler. Cleopatra III's brother is her cousin and her son because when you marry your uncle, your cousin is also your stepson.

This should be perfectly clear.

If you're Ptolemy VIII, then your wife is your stepdaughter, and you're her uncle and her husband because technically she's your niece because her mother is your sister. So, obviously, your wife's mother is your sister, your sister is your mother-in-law, and you are your own uncle.

PEOPLE CAESAR DATED
(A.K.A. CAESER'S CONQUESTS)

Caesar has such an active dating life, it's amazing he has any time left over to conquer the world. He dates several queens and even a few of his best friends' wives. His reputation for chasing women is so well known, the Roman army sings marching songs about it. At this point in his life, Caesar is becoming pretty bald, so his active dating life is inspiring news for balding men everywhere.*

....

*Ironically, "Caesar" originally comes from the Latin word for "hairy."

"I Came, I Saw, I Conquered"

Enough with the Nile pleasure cruises—you probably want to get back to some battles. Caesar does, too. After winning the Egyptian civil war and cavorting with Cleopatra on her luxury yacht, Caesar feels a hankering to get back down to the business of conquering the world. He marches north through Israel and Syria and fights a decisive battle with the king of Turkey. At the Battle of Zela on August 2, 47 BC, King Pharnaces II has twenty thousand soldiers, *twice* as many as Caesar. But this does not stop Caesar from routing Pharnaces and utterly annihilating the Turkish army. It takes Caesar all of five days to completely cook the kingdom of Turkey, prompting him to craft his immortal phrase *"Veni, vidi, vici."*—"I came, I saw, I conquered."

Caesar is now the conqueror of nations on three continents. He decides it's high time to return to Rome and do a victory dance. He needs to take a break from conquering the world, and spend some time actually running it. What Caesar doesn't know is that assassins await him in Rome. . . .

6

NOT ANOTHER CIVIL WAR

RETURNING TO ROME, Caesar's first order of business is to organize a triumph. A triumph is a great parade honoring a conquering general. Caesar is so inspired by the opulent splendor of Egypt, he decides he needs to throw the best parade ever, ever. If you are in Rome in September of 46 BC, you do not want to miss out.

Caesar's parade features a giraffe (which some amazed Roman spectators describe as "a camel-leopard with a really long neck and legs"). Forty elephants carry torches in their trunks. Conquered people from around the world march in chains. Arrive early for good seats, because Caesar hands out money and— better yet—free food to the cheering crowds.

At the center of it all, Caesar rides in a four-horse chariot, his face painted red like the Roman god Jupiter. In a triumph, it's Roman custom to have a slave ride in the chariot while holding a golden crown over the general's head and whispering to him that he will someday die. It's intended to keep the generals humble, though it's sort of a buzzkill.

You have a lot of entertainment choices during Caesar's party. Gladiator contests are held, along with a beast-hunt involving four hundred lions. If you find your way to the Field of Mars, there is an entire naval battle reenacted in a flooded basin. You can also visit the Circus Maximus, where two armies of war captives fight to the death. These armies are huge—each contains two thousand people, two hundred horses, and twenty elephants. They're all killed in the name of entertainment. Think about that: more people die at Caesar's party than are killed in the Falklands War and the Iranian Revolution combined. There is further bloodshed when a riot breaks out. Now you know it's a good party. Caesar restores calm by ordering priests to sacrifice two rioters on the Field of Mars. He rings up a huge tab for this shindig, but why not? As he is about to learn, life can be short. However, Caesar being Caesar, he finds a way to make time last a little longer.

Caesar Conquers Time

Caesar, realizing he hasn't conquered anyone in months, decides to conquer time itself. He makes 46 BC the longest year in history by adding three months to it. Up until this point, the Roman calendar is always incorrect—ten and a quarter days short of filling a year. But while on his Nile trip with Cleopatra, Caesar picks up a few handy tricks from the Egyptians, who are superior astronomers. Caesar fixes the Roman calendar to be 365 days divided into twelve months, with a leap day every four years. In his new calendar, the month of July is named after Julius Caesar, because it's the month of his birthday. Later, August will be named for his heir, Augustus.

Assassination

Caesar likes to work quickly and without a lot of back talk. Why does he need a pesky Senate to second-guess his brilliant ideas? As Finn Greenquill tells us in our weekly staff meetings, it's always easier to get things done when no one can tell you no.

Caesar has himself declared dictator for life on February 14, 44 BC. He doesn't know it yet, but his "lifelong dictatorship" is about to last all of one month. The Roman Senators—all members of Rome's upper class—are furious about losing the power and influence they've enjoyed for centuries. When you've got a dictator, who needs Senators? Nervous about Caesar's absolute power, a pack of Senators secretly plot his murder.

On the morning of March 15, 44 BC, Caesar's third wife, Calpurnia, has a premonition of his death. She asks him not to go to the Senate that morning and begs him to call in sick. Caesar rejects this idea—he's got an empire to run.

His good friend Brutus leads him to the Senate, and into a trap. Brutus, it should be mentioned, is the son of one of Caesar's girlfriends. Caesar is not only Brutus's friend, but he's pretty sure that he's Brutus's father. Nevertheless, Brutus and a fellow Senator, Cassius, are the ones to lead Caesar's assassination.

Get to the Roman Forum early, grab some fast food from a thermopolium, and find a comfortable spot to watch. Or just throw on a toga and join in—it's your call. When Caesar arrives at the Roman Forum, he is surrounded by sixty Senators who are in on the conspiracy, so you will have no trouble blending into the crowd. Caesar tries to fight back, but Senators crowd so close he is unable to draw his sword. The Senators try to share the task of killing him. Caesar is stabbed twenty-three times, because Senates can't do anything efficiently. Some believe Caesar doesn't give up fighting until he sees his own son Brutus stab him. That is the blow that breaks his heart.

PRANKING THE PAST

The beautiful part about mucking around in the past is creating alternative timelines. Want to transport Genghis Khan's pillaging army to the Super Bowl Halftime Show? Go right ahead! Want to give iridium blasters to the Founding Fathers at the Battle of Bunker Hill? Be our guest! Want to sneak an alligator into Ivan the Terrible's bathtub the night before the Massacre of Novgorod? Fantastic! After your vacation, the good people at Time Corp's Time Cleaners will erase all of your changes to the world's timeline.

Here are some ideas for pranking ancient Rome:

1. In AD 73, a Roman army of about 15,000 attacks 960 trapped rebels at Masada in Israel. It's a pretty unfair fight. Use your Time Corp Time Machine SE™ to transport a Tyrannosaurus rex behind Roman lines. This should even the score.

2. Three Roman legions sack Jerusalem in AD 70, destroying the city. Again, it's not really a fair fight. One Roman advantage is bronze armor and shielding. Use your time machine to freeze time. Then replace the Roman legions' armor with pink ballet leotards and tutus.

3. Install a metal detector at the Roman Senate in 44 BC and you can completely prevent Caesar's

Mark Antony

The Romans are into a lot of things—crucifixions, beheadings, assassinations—but they're especially into having civil wars. Someone needs to avenge Caesar's murder. And Mark Antony is the man for the job.

Mark Antony is a former cavalry officer and loyal friend of Caesar's.

He's youthful, handsome, square-jawed, and curly haired. Like Caesar, he dates all his friends' wives. He also likes to party. On one occasion, he attaches lions to a chariot and goes joyriding through Rome. On another occasion, he opens his mouth to speak in front of the Senate and vomits out all the remains of the wedding feast he'd had the night before.

But in avenging Caesar, Mark Antony seems to have finally found his purpose. He makes a funeral speech in the Forum for all the people of Rome to hear. He removes the bloody toga from Caesar's body and shows the crowd the twenty-three stab wounds. The Roman crowd is whipped up into their natural state—an angry mob. They burn down the Senate and then attack Brutus's and Cassius's houses. Brutus and Cassius flee to Greece and amass an army.

Mark Antony needs money and power to fight Brutus and Cassius's army and exact his revenge. So he forms an alliance with Caesar's adopted son, Octavian, and Caesar's trusted cavalry commander, Lepidus. Together, they have the political might to raise an army to avenge Caesar.

MARK ANTONY AND OCTAVIAN
PLOTTING REVENGE

Assassination of Cicero

You may think modern politicians are cutthroat, but in Rome the politicians will literally cut your throat. Mark Antony and his ally Octavian make a hit list of all the conspirators they need to kill to avenge Caesar. It's a long and impressive list, but near the top is a Senator named Cicero.

Cicero, the speaker of the Senate, bitterly opposes Mark Antony. He delivers a series of fiery speeches, denouncing Mark Antony and calling him an enemy of the state. He publicly proclaims his joy over Caesar's murder; his only regret is that Mark Antony was not murdered, too. Cicero is trying to rally the Roman mob against Antony, and Antony decides enough is enough.[*]

On the morning of December 7, 43 BC, a crow flies into Cicero's window and pecks at his bedcovers. Cicero takes this as a bad omen—a warning of misfortune. His servants carry him on a litter and race him through the woods to spirit him away to the sea and escape Rome. But Mark Antony's centurion assassin chases them down. Cicero pokes his head out of the silk curtains of his litter. You may not want to watch this next part. . . .

Cicero's last words are, "There is nothing proper about what you are doing, soldier, but do try to kill me properly." He bows his head to the centurion in a gladiatorial gesture to offer the soldier a clean stroke. Apparently, the centurion still requires three

---

[*]It's worth having lunch with Mark Antony, and with Cicero, just not at the same time.

blows and some sawing to completely lop off Cicero's head.[*] At Mark Antony's orders, the centurion chops off Cicero's hands, too—the hands that wrote those inflammatory speeches.[†]

Mark Antony puts Cicero's head on display, nailing it to the main podium in the Roman Forum. Antony's charming wife, Fulvia, spits on Cicero's face and repeatedly stabs his tongue with her hairpin, cursing Cicero's powers of speech.

If you are invited to dinner at Mark Antony's, just know that people claim he has Cicero's head placed on his dinner table during every meal, until it eventually becomes too rotten.

Antony and Octavian successfully work their way through their hit list, killing two thousand Romans, including one-third of the Senate. Now Antony and Octavian meet Caesar's final assassins on the field of battle.

Battle of Philippi

Brutus and Cassius raise an army of 187,000 soldiers in Greece. Mark Antony and Octavian pursue, arriving at the battlefield on October 23, 42 BC, with 223,000 soldiers.

If Mark Antony is the portrait of manliness, Octavian just simply isn't. He's so short he wears lifts in his shoes. He's constantly

---

[*]See "Helpful Hints" on page 60 for an important reminder of the first rule of time travel: do not get yourself beheaded. We really can't stress this enough.

[†]If you're feeling bad for Cicero at this point, we'd like to point out that he was something of a slumlord. When notified that two of his buildings had collapsed, Cicero's response was pleasure that he could rebuild and raise rents on the new tenants.

sneezing and coughing and getting sunstroke. He's late to the battle because he doesn't feel well. And whereas Mark Antony fights all over the battlefield, Octavian is so weak he gets carried around on a litter. Octavian gets so tired of being made fun of, he eventually passes a law preventing anyone from calling him "boy."

The Battle of Philippi is interesting to watch because the troops on both sides are Romans, equally matched in skill and weaponry. So the battle is decided by its generals. Mark Antony rallies his men to victory. The troops do not rely on long-range weapons like arrows and javelins. Rather, it is a bloody infantry fight, with close fighting, sword to sword. Brutus's troops break and run.

Realizing his failure, Brutus commits suicide by falling onto his own sword. Cassius had already thrown in the towel, ordering one of his own men to behead him. Mark Antony seems to like the beheading idea. When he finds Brutus's dead body on the battlefield, he orders the head to be lopped off and sent back to Rome to be put on display.* Somehow, the severed head is lost in the mail on the way to Rome and never found.†

Mark Antony Wins the Civil War

Rome is now ruled by Mark Antony and Octavian. Everything should go swimmingly from here on, right? What could possi-

....

*We told you, these Romans are crazy about decapitation.

†If you happen to find Brutus's head, Finn Greenquill will pay you good money for it.

bly go wrong? Surely there couldn't be any more decapitations on their way? There couldn't actually be another civil war coming down the pipe, could there?

A FRIENDLY MESSAGE FROM YOUR
CORPORATE OVERLORD
AT TIME CORP

Finn Greenquill here! My image consultants inform me that earlier in the book, I may have given the impression that I stole my time machine technology from my college roommate, Clarence. And that may not make me seem "likable" or "relatable" to the minions buying these books.

So let me be clear: I didn't *not* steal the time machine from Clarence. Nor am I admitting to denying stealing the time machine. I'm not saying I didn't do it. I'm just saying it could have been anyone.

In fact, who's to say Clarence didn't steal the time machine from me?

Okay, sure, Clarence is bankrupt and mining coal in a debtor's prison on Cirelius 5, while I am making quadrillions of dollars from a time machine business. I guess what I'm really saying is, there are a trillion people in the universe . . . so the odds that I'm the one person who actually stole the time machine are literally one in a trillion.

In the end, we all benefit from time travel. So didn't we *all* steal the time machine? Think about it.

Finn Greenquill

Corporate Overlord, Time Corp

7

ANTONY AND CLEOPATRA

THE TIME OF Antony and Cleopatra is one of Time Corp's most popular vacation packages. It's 41 BC, and Mark Antony's just won the civil war. But his real problems have only just begun. Iran (called Parthia at the time) is invading Roman territory and becoming a thorn in the side of Rome. Antony decides it's high time to do some conquering. First things first: if Antony's going to attack Parthia, he's going to need money. Lots of it. So he sails east to meet the richest person in the world: Cleopatra.

Sail with Antony's fleet to Tarsus, where he summons Cleopatra from Alexandria. Cleopatra makes him wait a few days before she actually shows up, just to prove she doesn't take orders from Romans. You can skip the long wait because you have a time machine. But you won't want to miss her big entrance. . . .

Cleopatra's royal barge, with purple sails unfurled, is rowed by 167 slaves pulling silver oars to the rhythmic music of flutes, fifes, and harps. Cleopatra poses under a canopy of golden cloth,

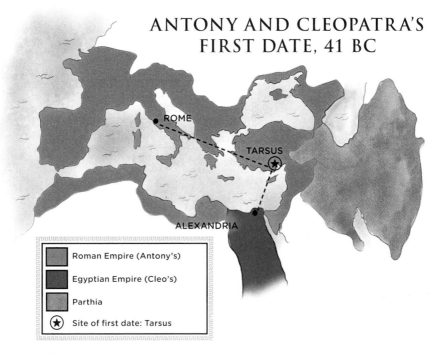

ANTONY AND CLEOPATRA'S FIRST DATE, 41 BC

ROME

TARSUS ⊛

ALEXANDRIA

Roman Empire (Antony's)

Egyptian Empire (Cleo's)

Parthia

⊛ Site of first date: Tarsus

dressed as the goddess Venus, and is fanned with palm fronds by young boys dressed up like cupids. Her maids, costumed like sea nymphs, steer the rudder and work the ropes.

Antony sends Cleopatra a dinner invitation. But Cleopatra is the queen of Egypt; she isn't at anyone's beck and call. She declines Antony's invitation and invites him to dinner instead. It's a power move. Antony, a mere Roman, has never before witnessed Egypt's wealth. Rome is still a young empire and not nearly as decadent as Egypt. When Antony shows up for dinner on Cleo's barge, he is treated to the most expensive feast he's ever seen. If you can sneak into this dinner, we recommend it.

Thousands of lights are hung from tree branches, the air is scented with perfume, and the walls are hung with priceless tapestries. Rose petals drop throughout the meal until the floor is carpeted 18 inches deep. The flower bill alone comes to 75 pounds of gold. Cleopatra apologizes for not having enough time to prepare a really elegant feast. Antony tries to pick his jaw up off the floor.

Cleopatra gestures to the lavish display and tells Antony that if he likes the decorations, he should take them all home with him. Antony leaves the dinner party with jewel-encrusted dishware and couches laden with silks. The two monarchs continue to meet every night for dinner, and soon they are inseparable. Antony has a war raging in Syria and fierce political battles in Rome, but he abandons everything to return to Egypt with Cleopatra. She needs his army to build her empire, and he needs her wealth to fund his war on Parthia. But besides all of that, Antony is smitten.

HELPFUL HINTS: IF YOU ARE INVITED TO A ROMAN DINNER PARTY

The great thing about ancient Rome is that *every* party is a toga party. Plus, Romans love to eat. There are more than three hundred restaurants in Pompeii alone,* from fast food to elegant dining. If you get invited to a Roman dinner party, bring your appetite. A dinner party can last from 2:00 p.m. until late into the night.

Dinner is served in three courses: an appetizer, a main course, and dessert. Here is a sample menu of actual popular Roman recipes. You are in luck— mice are a Roman delicacy!

Appetizer

Dormouse sprinkled with poppy seed and honey and served with hot sausages on a silver gridiron, on a bed of damson plums and pomegranate seeds

*A word to the wise: if you visit Pompeii, be sure to arrive before August 24, AD 79, when Mount Vesuvius erupts, cooking the inhabitants in a blast of 500 degree heat and burying the entire town under 20 feet of volcanic ash. Also, if you see Pliny the Elder heading toward Pompeii, tell him he is better off staying home with a good book.

At a Roman dinner party, guests recline on couches with their left arms propped on a cushion. The couches surround a low dinner table. Discarded food and bones are tossed on the floor for servants to clean up. Musicians, poets, dancers, or acrobats often entertain the diners.

Partying with Antony and Cleopatra

Mark Antony and Cleopatra cavort around the streets of Alexandria. They do everything together—they drink wine, play dice, hunt, and go to parties. At night, they disguise themselves as common servants, knock loudly on people's doors, and run away laughing. At one party, Cleopatra playfully bets Antony that she can spend ten million sesterces on a single dinner. She serves him a simple dinner, after which she removes one priceless pearl earring, dissolves it in a cup of vinegar, and drinks it down.[*]

....

[*]The real headline here is not that Cleopatra was willing to destroy expensive pearls, but that she was willing to drink a glass of vinegar.

Antony is besotted with Cleopatra. To show her how much he cares, he does what anyone would—he helps her assassinate the rest of her siblings. Cleopatra still has a remaining brother and sister running around making claims on her throne, so Antony executes them. After all, this is true love.

Marriage

On December 25, 40 BC, Cleopatra gives birth to Antony's twins, Alexander Helios and Cleopatra Selene II. Soon after, Antony decides to make Egypt his permanent home.

This is a gutsy move on Mark Antony's part, because he is currently married to his ally Octavian's sister.* Not to worry. He quickly divorces Octavian's sister and marries Cleopatra. This causes a major scandal in Rome, which really doesn't bother Mark Antony because he's in Egypt. He and Cleo soon have a third child, Ptolemy Philadelphus.

....

*You may remember Fulvia, Mark Antony's charming wife who spit on Cicero's de-capitated head? Well, amazingly, that marriage didn't work out. For political rea-sons, Mark Antony married Octavian's sister, whose name is . . . are you ready . . . Octavia. She is Mark Antony's *fourth* marriage. That makes Cleopatra his *fifth* mar-riage. But hey, maybe the fifth time's the charm.

HELPFUL HINTS: ROMAN WEDDINGS

If you're invited to a Roman wedding, here are some tips on Roman customs.

- The bride will wear a wedding dress with a veil. But the veil is reddish-orange rather than white.
- The bride wears an iron ring on the middle finger of her left hand. This is because Roman physicians incorrectly believe there is a nerve in the third finger that leads directly to the heart.
- The bride says a wedding vow, but the groom does not.
- A feast is held at the bride's house. Then there's a parade to the groom's house, during which the crowd throws nuts. A young boy carries a flaming wedding torch, which the bride will eventually chuck into the crowd. Don't worry, the bride snuffs it out first. If you're lucky enough to catch this torch, you will have good luck and a long life.
- Finally, the groom's friends pick up the bride and carry her across the threshold of the groom's house. This spares the groom the risk of throwing his back out. Once the bride is married, she continues to be the property of her father and enjoys very few legal rights. It's all very romantic!

Antony and Cleopatra Divide Up the World

All parents want to give the world to their children. Few parents actually do. In 34 BC, Cleopatra and her son Caesarion are crowned co-rulers of Egypt and Cyprus. Antony and Cleopatra give their older son, Alexander Helios, the kingdom of Armenia, Iran, and Central Asia. They give a wonderful little gift to their daughter, Cleopatra Selene II: the country of Libya. To their younger son, Ptolemy Philadelphus, they give Lebanon, Syria, and Turkey.

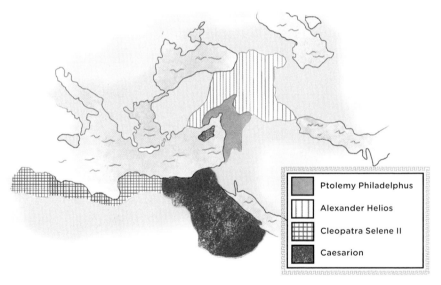

Ptolemy Philadelphus
Alexander Helios
Cleopatra Selene II
Caesarion

The people of Rome decide that enough is enough. Mark Antony is giving away the entire Roman Empire to his Egyptian queen's kids. The Roman Senate sends Octavian to battle against Mark Antony. That's right—it's time for *another* civil war!

HANNIBAL

While we're on the topic of people trying to ruin the Roman Empire, this is as good a time as any to meet one of the greatest generals of all time: Hannibal. Hannibal kills more Romans than anyone else in history, including the Romans. He is from Carthage, a port in North Africa just across the water from Sicily.

Hannibal's father is the leading general in Carthage's first war with Rome, in the third century BC. When Hannibal is nine, his father holds him over a fire and makes him swear he will fight and destroy Rome. Young Hannibal readily agrees. So his father takes him to war in Spain, and Hannibal devotes the next seventeen years of his life to battle training.

After his father is drowned and his brother assassinated, Hannibal becomes commander of the Carthaginian forces. He promptly conquers Spain and marches his army through France and across the Alps to attack Italy. If you've ever tried to march one hundred thousand soldiers and forty war elephants over an ice-covered mountain range while being attacked by wild mountain men, you know it's easier said than done. The march is so treacherous, Hannibal loses all but one of his elephants, and even loses his own right eye. But when he arrives in Italy, ready for battle, the Romans are stunned and completely unprepared.

Hannibal proceeds to wipe the floor with the Roman army. Within the next twenty months alone, he kills 150,000 Roman soldiers in combat, roughly 20 percent of all the men in Italy. Not too shabby.

Hannibal's masterpiece is the Battle of Cannae. He feigns a retreat, luring the Romans to plunge headlong into his forces. The Carthaginians then surround the Romans, trapping them in a kill box. Between fifty thousand and seventy thousand Romans are killed. This means Carthaginians are butchering Romans at a rate of one hundred per minute for eight hours. This is the bloodiest battle in antiquity, and that's saying something.

Ultimately, the only thing that can stop Hannibal is bureaucracy. Despite all of his successes, the Carthaginian government treats Hannibal like chopped liver, and does a pretty shoddy job of sending him fresh troops, money, food, or weapons. Miraculously, Hannibal continues to devastate Rome, winning nearly every battle he fights for the next seventeen years. But eventually his troops are exhausted, aging, and running out of supplies. Hannibal is called back to Africa, and finally beaten by the Roman general Scipio Africanus at the Battle of Zama, near Carthage.

If you have lunch with Hannibal, choose your words carefully. He can be a bit touchy.

HELPFUL HINTS: THE INVERSE ELEPHANT LAW

If history is any guide, whichever army has the most elephants always loses in the end.

The Inverse Elephant Law

$$\text{Whereby if } \frac{1}{(x)\text{Elephants}_{(Army1)}} > \frac{1}{(y)\text{Elephants}_{(Army2)}} \text{ Army 1 wins}$$

Army elephants always seem like a good idea at the time. Elephants charge at 20 miles per hour. They have thick hides to repel arrows. And a line of infantry spears that can stop a horse charge in its tracks won't even cause an elephant to bat an eye. Elephants are also quite useful for torture. Hannibal likes to lay prisoners on the ground, place an elephant's foot on their chest, and have the elephants slowly crush the prisoners to death.

All this is well and good, but toss an elephant into a battle, and you may suddenly have a 6-ton headache on your hands. Elephants, as it happens, don't like getting pelted with javelins. They are quite liable to turn tail and charge, rampaging, back into their own lines.

In Hannibal's last stand against Roman general Scipio Africanus, elephants may have been Hannibal's downfall. For starters, a good portion of Han-

nibal's eighty war elephants were only recently captured from the wild, and not particularly tame (wild
elephants being slightly more dangerous for an army
than tame elephants).

When Hannibal charged his elephants at the Romans, they were greeted by Roman trumpeters,
which drove many confused elephants into a fearful
retreat, crashing right back into the Carthaginian

cavalry. Several of the elephants did manage to charge in the correct direction, but were goaded harmlessly through the loose Roman ranks by well-trained infantry. The remaining elephants became so peeved by Roman javelins, they left the battlefield in a huff, inconveniently trampling the Carthaginian infantry along their way.

The Battle of Actium

Set your time machine for September 2, 31 BC, for the Battle of Actium in Greece. Octavian's decided Rome has gone far too

long without a proper civil war. His fleet blockades Antony and Cleopatra's navy so they cannot escape the Greek shore. Octavian needs to conquer Antony's troops so he can win back all the Roman lands Antony squandered on Cleopatra's kids. Antony delays the battle as long as he can, but his troops are low on food and water and dying of malaria. With no other way to escape, he attacks Octavian's fleet head-on.

Mark Antony is outnumbered, but his fleet contains massive war galleys weighing 250 tons. These ships are armed with huge rams and high towers loaded with archers. In the height of the battle, when they are supposed to attack, Cleopatra's ships flee instead. She prefers to make a getaway. So she ditches Antony's navy, leaving him holding the bag. There's love for you.

Antony, bewildered, sacrifices two-thirds of his fleet, and all of his ground forces, to chase after Cleopatra. He leaves nearly all of his men behind and thus, in one battle, loses all of his military strength. Antony pursues Cleopatra all the way across the Mediterranean Sea.

When Cleopatra reaches Egypt, she battens down the hatches and prepares for Octavian to attack. Her first order of business is to raise a bunch of money. She goes on a killing spree, assassinating all her wealthy rivals and taking their money.

Next, Cleopatra tries to find military allies. She's kept the king of Armenia locked in a dungeon with golden chains for three years. She cuts off his head* and sends it to his enemy, the king of the Medes. But despite this compelling gift, the king of the Medes doesn't come to Cleopatra's aid. Her other ally, King Herod, a charming man who orders two of his sons to be strangled and drowns his own brother-in-law in a swimming pool, abandons Cleopatra and becomes allies with Octavian.

With no remaining friends, Cleopatra makes plans to escape to India. She orders slaves to haul her Mediterranean ships 40 miles across the land to get to the Red Sea. The ships are 300 feet long and 60 feet high. It's a schlep. But when the slaves finally manage to haul the ships to the Red Sea, Egyptian rebels set fire to the entire fleet.

Cleopatra forms a new plan. She stuffs all the money, spices, and treasure she can find into a giant mausoleum she builds in Alexandria. Her slaves fill the building with kindling. Cleopatra

....
*We promised you more decapitation and we delivered.

locks herself inside and sends word to Octavian that she'll burn all of Egypt's money if he attacks her. Meanwhile, she begins experimenting with poisons on her prisoners to see which venoms kill most effectively, with the least amount of pain.

Antony gallantly sends word to Octavian that he will kill himself if it means Octavian will spare Cleopatra's life. He's still in love and willing to die for her. Octavian rejects the offer.

Antony raises a few remaining troops and watches from the shore as his fleet sails out to battle the Roman navy. To Antony's dismay, his entire navy switches sides, joining the Romans. Next, Antony's cavalry gallops onto the battlefield, crosses to the other side, and joins the Romans as well. Finally, Antony's infantry march onto the battlefield, give a halfhearted fight, and quickly lose.

Antony angrily returns to Alexandria and shuts himself up in his room. He tries to kill himself, but manages to bungle it. He falls on his sword, misses the correct ribs, and pierces his abdomen. It's just one of those days. He's now dying in the most slow and painful way possible.

Cleopatra hears the outcry from her window. She realizes Antony is dying. Overcome by emotion, she sends her servants to fetch him. Since her mausoleum is locked tight, Cleopatra lowers ropes from her second-story window and hauls Antony up through her window. Reunited at last, she wipes the blood from his body, smears it on her face, and says, "Oh, my master, my commander, my husband." Antony dies in her arms.

Cleopatra and her servants then kill themselves by clasping a deadly cobra to their chests. By the time Octavian's soldiers break down the door of Cleopatra's mausoleum, they find her lying dead on a golden couch. She is wearing her most expensive silks, and her hands grip her crook and flail—the symbols of an Egyptian pharaoh.

Octavian is thrilled Cleopatra didn't get the chance to set fire to all the treasure in the mausoleum. He summons the *psylli*, snake charmers from North Africa, famous for their ability to save people from lethal snake bites. He was hoping to capture Cleopatra alive so he could march her in chains through the streets of Rome. That would have been icing on the cake. But Cleopatra is long dead. The moral here is to always think twice before entering politics.

8

ROME'S TOP FIVE CRAZIEST EMPERORS

OCTAVIAN NOW CONTROLS Rome and all its territories. The Senate grants him the honorary title of "Augustus" and crowns him an emperor. No longer will Rome be ruled by elected consuls and voting Senators. Sorry, democracy. Rome is now an empire and will be under the thumb of unelected emperors for the next few centuries. True democracy will not be seen again for nearly two thousand years, when a cluster of relatively insignificant British colonies band together and declare themselves the United States of America.

So let's talk about the Roman emperors. You may think you're a fairly nice, kind, regular person, but that's just because no one's given you unlimited wealth and power yet. To give a taste of just how crazy a person can get with unlimited wealth and power, here are five of Rome's most insane emperors and empresses. Feel free to visit each of them; just be very, very careful to stay on their good sides.

CALIGULA
Born August 31, AD 12, Anzio, Italy
Assassinated January 24, AD 41 (age 28)

Caligula anoints his favorite horse, Galloper, to be a priest, and then attempts to make the horse a Senator. He spends a lavish amount of public money building Galloper a marble stable, complete with chairs and couches that the horse is never known to sit in. Caligula then invites important guests over to have dinner with Galloper. See if you can score an invitation! Then write a letter to Time Corp and let us know if it's as weird as we imagine.

When Caligula is young, a fortune-teller predicts he is more likely to ride his horse across water than to become emperor. So upon ascending the throne, Caligula orders a group of ships to be lashed together, forming a pontoon bridge across the Bay of Naples. Caligula then rides Galloper across the entire bay and throws an enormous banquet.

Caligula loves to attend gladiator matches. On one occasion, the games run out of criminals to feed to the wild beasts. So

Caligula orders his bodyguards to yank spectators into the arena and feed them to the lions for his amusement.

Caligula is very vain. He often practices grimacing in front of the mirror, to look mean. And he makes it a crime for anyone to look at his bald spot.

He is finally assassinated by his bodyguards and a flock of Senators as he crosses through an alleyway. He has ruled for four years.

VALERIA MESSALINA
Born January 25, AD 20, Rome
Executed AD 48, Gardens of Lucullus, Rome (age 28)

Valeria Messalina is an empress so messed up, she puts the "mess" in Valeria Messalina.* She is Caligula's cousin, so she really doesn't have great genes to begin with.

....
*Finn Greenquill forced us to include that sentence. It was his idea, not ours.

Valeria becomes empress after she marries Emperor Claudius in AD 37. He's at least thirty years older than her, but who's counting? Claudius is so pleased with seventeen-year-old Messalina that he does anything she wants, including exiling or executing anyone who displeases her. This, it turns out, is quite a long list.

The problem with Messalina is that despite being the empress, she dates everyone in Rome. Her reputation puts Caesar and Mark Antony to shame.

Eventually, Messalina marries a Senator, Gaius Silius, while Emperor Claudius is out of town on a business trip. She then persuades Silius to divorce his wife. That accomplished, Silius and Messalina plan to overthrow Claudius and make Silius emperor. The idea turns out to be, well, a bit silius. Claudius's staff discovers the plot and executes Messalina and Silius.

JULIA AGRIPPINA
Born November 7, AD 15, Cologne
Assassinated AD 59, Misenum (age 43)

Agrippina is Emperor Claudius's fourth wife and his niece. She is very beautiful, but let's not sugarcoat it—she's a serial killer. By all accounts she seduces her uncle Claudius, and then uses her new-found powers as empress to fuel a reign of terror. Here is a list of people she is rumored to have murdered in her seven years as empress:

- **Passienus Crispus. Poisoned.** Agrippina's second husband (Claudius was her third husband).

- **Lollia Paulina. Forced to commit suicide.** A rival for Claudius's hand in marriage.

- **Lucius Silanus. Committed suicide.** Betrothed to Octavia, Claudius's daughter. Agrippina didn't approve of the match, and so on his wedding day spread rumors to dishonor him.

- **Sosibius. Executed.** Tutor of Britannicus, Claudius's son. Plotted against Agrippina's son, Nero.

- **Calpurnia. Executed.** Claudius commented on her beauty.

- **Statilius Taurus. Forced to commit suicide.** Agrippina wanted his gardens.

- **Emperor Claudius. Poisoned.** Her husband.

- **Domitia Lepida. Executed.** Messalina's mother.

- **Marcus Junius Silanus. Poisoned.** Potential rival to Agrippina's son, Nero.

- **Cadius Rufus. Executed.** Accused of extortion.

Eventually, Agrippina's son, Nero, tries to kill her by sending her sailing on a sinking ship. It's rumored he also tries to kill her by having the ceiling of her bedroom collapse. And he may also try poisoning her several times. It's difficult to keep track. After she keeps surviving, Nero eventually hires three assassins who kill her and make it look like a suicide.

NERO
Born December 15, AD 37, Anzio, Italy
Honor Suicide, June 9, AD 68 (age 30)

If you've got some killing to do, it doesn't hurt to be a Roman emperor. Nero, in particular, seems to have a few issues with women. As you know, he kills his mother, Agrippina. Next, he beheads his first wife. Then he gives his first wife's head to his second wife, Poppaea, so she can gloat. But surprisingly, his relationship with Poppaea doesn't work out either. Not to put too fine a point on it, but Nero eventually kicks her to death.

Nero considers himself a master of all trades. He competes in the 67 Olympics, racing a ten-horse chariot. But before you place any bets, we should mention that Nero bribed the Olympic judges. Despite spectacularly crashing his chariot, Nero takes home several Olympic medals.

Nero also enjoys singing in public, often while parading through the streets of Rome in an open wagon. According to some, Nero's singing is his greatest crime against humanity. That may not be the case, however. Nero also commissions a 120-foot bronze statue of himself, completely naked, and places it on a hill overlooking the entire city.

Rome catches fire on July 18, AD 64. The fire rages for six days, destroying much of the city. You might want to schedule your trip around that—although you can catch a decent price on some prime riverfront property once the fire simmers down. Nero, in need of a scapegoat, blames the Christians, and orders them burned, crucified, and fed to the dogs. Perhaps at this point, Nero could have done with some good advice. But unfortunately, he ordered his adviser, the famous philosopher Seneca, to slit his wrists in a bathtub.

Faced with the enormous cost of rebuilding Rome after the fire, Nero strikes upon a brilliant idea. He forces rich men to name him as their heir, and then forces them to kill themselves. This is all a bit much, even for Romans. But Nero really crosses the line when he decides to raise taxes.

At this, the Romans decide they've had enough. The people revolt and Nero's bodyguards desert him. The Senate, in a landmark decision, votes to beat Nero to death. Nero has slaves dig his grave for him, and then orders his secretary to cut his throat for him. His last words are, "Oh, what an artist the world is losing!"

COMMODUS
Born August 31, AD 161, Lanuvium, near Rome
Assassinated December 31, AD 192 (age 31)

Commodus is a man who likes to get things done. At one point, he orders all the cripples, hunchbacks, and homeless in Rome to be rounded up, herded into the Colosseum, and forced to chop each other to death with meat cleavers.

Commodus is many things, but he is not an animal lover. From the safe height of a podium in the Colosseum, Commodus kills one hundred lions in a single day. It's actually somewhat impressive because he performs this feat with only one hundred spears. For a finishing touch, he kills three elephants, spears a giraffe, and beheads an ostrich. The entire Senate is present for this spectacle. The ASPCA, however, is not.

The Senate successfully poisons Commodus's dinner, but he throws it all up and survives. So the Senate convinces Commodus's wrestling coach, a gladiator named Narcissus, to strangle Commodus while he is taking a bath. Commodus rules for twelve years. Cause of death? Strangled in the bath by a wrestler.

HELPFUL HINTS: REMEMBERING ALL THE ROMAN EMPERORS

All told, there were 147 Roman emperors. Confused about how to remember the number of Roman emperors? Here's a simple trick.

Just think of the number of major gods according to the Roman historian Varro, 20, divided by the number of major gods according to the Roman historian Livy, 12, multiplied by the number of Romans in Augustus's Senate, 600, divided by the mathematical constant π times the mathematical constant e where e is defined as:

$$e=\sum \frac{1}{n!} = 1 + \frac{1}{1} + \frac{1}{1*2} + \frac{1}{1*2*3} \cdots$$

divided by the number of Roman soldiers in a *centuria*, 100, raised to the power of 3, for the Roman triumvirate, round to the nearest integer, and subtract 500, and you have the answer: 147!

Becoming a Roman Emperor

We know what you're thinking. Why should these emperors have all the fun? *You* could be a Roman emperor. Wealth, lands, and power beyond reckoning. And with your godlike powers as a time traveler armed with an iridium blaster, becoming emperor should be a mere walk in the park.

Well, consider this. Julius Caesar effectively abolishes Roman democracy, so there's no way for Romans to vote out leaders who become unpopular. The only method of regime change is assassination. Caesar set the precedent, getting himself assassinated after only one month on the job. For the next three hundred years, assassinating emperors is all Roman citizens seem to do with their time.

Assassination becomes such a problem that in the fifty years from AD 235 to AD 284, Rome has a whopping twenty-six different emperors.

KNOWN CAUSES OF DEATH OF ROMAN EMPERORS
AUGUSTUS THROUGH CONSTANTINE XI PALAIOLOGOS

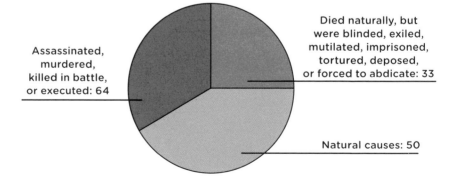

Assassinated, murdered, killed in battle, or executed: 64

Died naturally, but were blinded, exiled, mutilated, imprisoned, tortured, deposed, or forced to abdicate: 33

Natural causes: 50

Surviving Assassination

If you simply must become the emperor of Rome, you will probably survive a bit longer if you don't behave like an absolute monster. Still, you never know when the Roman mob will grow tired of your antics. Here are a few handy tidbits on not getting yourself assassinated.

Poisoning, and How to Avoid It

Poison is all the rage in ancient Rome. Nero poisons so many of his relatives at the dinner table that he hires his own royal poisoner, a woman named Locusta. Nero's personal favorite poison is cyanide. Colorless, odorless, and pretty tasteless.

Nero's predecessor, Emperor Claudius, was fed poisonous mushrooms. There were enough people at his last dinner party that no one has entirely solved the mystery of who killed Claudius. Some believe it was his doctor, Xenophon; some believe it was

Claudius's wife Agrippina. It may also have been Locusta, the royal poisoner, who later worked for Nero. Ironically, Claudius may actually have been poisoned by Halotus, the man hired to taste his food to make sure it wasn't poisoned. If you can score an invitation to this dinner, do history a favor and try to solve this ancient mystery.

The best way to avoid death by poisoning is developed by the Turkish king Mithridates the Great. Mithridates lives in constant fear of assassination, both from Romans and from his own people. (His son was whopped by Caesar at the Battle of Zela, where Caesar said, "I came, I saw, I conquered.") At night, Mithridates sleeps with a horse, a bull, and a stag in his bedroom, who will supposedly whinny, bellow, or bleat if anyone approaches his bed. He is so paranoid about being poisoned that he ingests trace amounts of poisons every day to develop immunities. Modern science shows that "Mithridatism" actually works for certain types of poisons, like snake venom, and can even be used to treat peanut allergies.

Assassination by the Praetorian Guard

A very popular method of assassination in Rome is to be killed by your own bodyguards. The Praetorian Guard are the most elite troops in the Roman military, responsible for protecting the emperor. The Praetorian Guard are known to have assassinated Caligula, Commodus, and at least twelve other emperors.

If you want to avoid being assassinated by your Praetorian Guard, maybe tip them once in a while. And would it kill you to give them a little something extra around the holidays?

Assassination by Roman Legion

If the Praetorian Guard doesn't turn on you, the Roman legions might. Many Roman emperors are ousted by a full-on civil war. The Roman legions fight in phalanx formation, interlocking shields. The phalanx is nearly invulnerable to attacks from arrows, spears, or swords. Each heavy infantryman is armed with swords, spears, pikes, or sarissas (incredibly long, 20-foot spears). Being attacked by a Roman legion will not be the most wonderful day of your life.

Perhaps the most important asset of the Roman legion is discipline. Remember on page 63 when Crassus punishes his legions with "decimation?" Decimation is a perfect example of Roman army discipline. If a regiment of soldiers attempts mutiny, desertion, or cowardice, they are split into groups of ten and forced to draw lots. The one man in each group who draws the odd lot is beaten to death by the other nine . . . with their bare hands. Thus, one-tenth of the army is wiped out.

Legionaries do not crack under pressure. They will climb their own dead to breach the wall of a fort. Keep in mind, Julius Caesar conquers most of Europe with only one hundred thousand of these lovely people.

For its time period, the Roman legion has many strengths and few vulnerabilities. If you find yourself attacked by a phalanx formation, consider using iridium lasers or a heat ray. Or simply transport the phalanx to a different part of history, like a Walmart parking lot in Decatur, Illinois. Other options include sending the Roman legion to the Macy's Thanksgiving Day Parade, or to the opening ceremony of the 1998 Winter Olympics in Nagano, Japan.

Beyond that, all we can do is wish you good luck and recommend one of Time Corp's very affordable life insurance policies. *Bon voyage!*

The Fall of the Roman Empire

If you're going to vacation in Rome during its fall, it's best to have good travel insurance and a real hankering to pillage. Most time travelers are reluctant to visit the late Roman Empire—it's simply too dangerous. The odds of getting attacked by rampaging Goths, Vandals, Huns, and other barbarians are outrageously high. That's why you will find Time Corp's prices to be outrageously low!

Try our discount package! Leave any Monday and return the previous Friday. That way you don't miss the weekend.

Curtains Time for Rome

Well, it was fun while it lasted. Without great leadership, Rome becomes an increasingly unpleasant place to live. There is a fifty-year period from AD 235 to AD 284 known simply as "The Age of Chaos" due to the incessant coups, assassinations, revolts, plagues, fires, and persecutions. It gets worse from there.

In AD 410, Visigoth barbarians arrive and sack the city of Rome, making off with all the loot and most of the decent table settings. As if that's not enough, Hun barbarians attack the rest of the empire. Adding insult to injury, Vandal barbarians turn up in AD 455 and sack the city all over again, taking everything the Visigoths didn't want. In AD 476, the last Roman emperor is deposed by the barbarian general Odoacer. The city and empire fall into ruin. It's a sad day for Rome, but on the bright side, Odoacer has a fantastic mustache.

So Long, and Thanks for All Your Money

We hope you've enjoyed your vacation in ancient Rome. If you have contracted malaria, been slaughtered by barbarians, or been otherwise inconvenienced, Time Corp would like to remind you that you signed a waiver. So it's really out of our hands.

Time Corp would also like to proudly announce that we only lost seventeen travel writers while researching for this guidebook. This is a huge improvement over our *Thrifty Guide to Prehistory*, in which we lost eighteen travel writers to velociraptors alone.

If for any reason you are not completely satisfied by your Time Corp Time Travel Vacation, we suggest you try Time Travel Vacations from Time Enterprises, a division of Time Corp.

Either way, we look forward, and backward, to hosting you on your next time traveling adventure.

Finn Greenquill here—you all know me. I wanted to take a moment to thank you for purchasing your amazingly affordable time travel package with Time Corp. Your money will go toward funding several very important causes.

First off, a portion of every purchase goes to supporting my diamond mining colony on Cirelius 5. Those diamonds don't mine themselves! And someone has to feed my diamond miners, at least a few times per week. Unions, am I right?

But your money does far more than build my massive diamond collection. It also goes to save endangered animal species in the wild, which my four-star chefs then catch, cook, and serve me in my floating glass restaurant orbiting Jupiter.

But I am not just about giant diamonds and flambéed endangered species. I am a person who truly cares about important causes. That is why I personally donate a portion of every Time Corp purchase to building my intergalactic space yacht. It has six hundred rooms, at least half of which are devoted to storing my immense diamond collection. There are also several swimming pools, which are particularly fun in the zero gravity of space. There is even an entire deck devoted to zero-gravity fox hunting.

I hope you all feel even better about the premium Time Corp time travel packages you've purchased, now that you know more about the important causes you are supporting. Safe travels, and we'll see you on your next adventure through time.

Finn Greenquill

Founder and Corporate Overlord, Time Corp

Bibliography

Aldrete, Gregory S. *Daily Life in the Roman City: Rome, Pompeii, and Ostia*. Daily Life Through History. Westport, Conn.: The Greenwood Press, 2004.

Appian. *The Civil Wars*. Translated with an introduction by John Carter. New York: Penguin Classics, 1997.

Caesar, Julius. *The Civil War*. Penguin Classics. Translated with an introduction by Jane P. Gardner. London: Penguin Books, 1967.

Caesar, Julius. *The Conquest of Gaul*. Penguin Classics. Translated with an introduction by Jane P. Gardner. London: Penguin Books, 1983.

Cicero. *Selected Political Speeches*. Translated with an introduction by Michael Grant. New York: Penguin Classics, 1977.

Pliny the Elder. *Natural History: A Selection*. Translated with an introduction by John F. Healey. New York: Penguin Classics, 1991.

Plutarch. *Life of Crassus*. Translated by Aubrey Stewart and George Long. London: George Bell & Sons, 1892.

Schiff, Stacy. *Cleopatra: A Life*. New York: Back Bay Books, 2011.

Acknowledgments

The travel writers at Time Corp would like to thank Julius Caesar for his hospitality, Mark Antony for his generous help with research, and Hannibal for not killing us. We would also like to thank Finn Greenquill, but we just can't bring ourselves to do it.

Thank you to art director Jim Hoover, designer Mariam Quraishi, and copy editor Janet Pascal, who knows more about ancient Rome than the ancient Romans.

A very special thank-you to Leila Sales, who is an editor at Viking but is not an actual Viking. Many heartfelt thanks to Brianne Johnson and Scott Carr, who are also not Vikings. A hearty tip of the hat to time traveler Zach Greenberger, who is not a Viking but can pass for one.

Jonathan W. Stokes is a former teacher turned Hollywood screenwriter, who has written screenplays for Warner Brothers, Universal, Fox, Paramount, New Line, and Sony/Columbia. Inspired by a childhood love of *The Goonies* and *Ferris Bueller's Day Off*, Jonathan writes the Addison Cooke series as well as the other books in the Thrifty Guide series. Raised in Connecticut, he currently resides in Los Angeles, where he can be found showing off his incredible taste in dishware and impressive 96 percent accuracy with high fives.

David Sossella graduated with honors in painting at the Accademia di Belle Arti in Venice. Since 2006, he's been illustrator and head of graphics for the largest animation studio in Italy.